SETON HALL UNIVERSITY

D0882673

JUL 24 1994

Family Therapy
With the
Elderly

Elizabeth R. Neidhardt
Jo Ann Allen

Sage Sourcebooks for
the Human Services Series
22

SETON HALL UNIVERSITY
McLA... ...RARY

SAGE Publications
International Educational and Professional Publisher
Newbury Park   London   New Delhi

Copyright © 1993 by Sage Publications, Inc.

All rights reserved. No part of this book may be reproduced or utilized in any form or by any means, electronic or mechanical, including photocopying, recording, or by any information storage and retrieval system, without permission in writing from the publisher.

For information address:

SAGE Publications, Inc.
2455 Teller Road
Newbury Park, California 91320

SAGE Publications Ltd.
6 Bonhill Street
London EC2A 4PU
United Kingdom

SAGE Publications India Pvt. Ltd.
M-32 Market
Greater Kailash I
New Delhi 110 048 India

Printed in the United States of America

Library of Congress Cataloging-in-Publication Data

Neidhardt, Elizabeth R.
　　Family therapy with the elderly / Elizabeth R. Neidhardt, Jo Ann Allen.
　　　　p. cm.—(SSHS : 22)
　　Includes bibliographical references and index.
　　ISBN 0-8039-4498-5 (cl).—ISBN 0-8039-4499-3 (pb)
　　1. Aged—Mental health. 2. Family psychotherapy. I. Allen, Jo Ann, II. Title. III. Series: Sage sourcebooks for the human services series: 22.
　　[DNLM: 1. Aged—pyschology. 2. Family therapy—in old age. 3. Family Therapy—methods. WM 430.5.F2 N397f]
　　RC451.4.A5N45　1993
　　618.97'689156—dc20
　　DNLM/DLC　　　　　　　　　　　　　　　　　　　92-49538

93　94　95　96　10　9　8　7　6　5　4　3　2　1

Sage Production Editor: Diane S. Foster

CONTENTS

INTRODUCTION

Demographic projections point to there being an increasing number of older people in American society. Some writers, noting that approximately 20% of the population will be over age 65 by the year 2000, refer to the graying of America. While an increased life span is cause for celebration, the growing number of older people raises special issues and concerns that our society is just beginning to understand and to address. Not only will the expansion of this segment of our population require a parallel burgeoning of services, but also the exact nature of these services is as yet unclear. Certainly human service providers are called upon to be part of this movement in their various roles as clinicians, educators, administrators, and policymakers. Many social workers are currently involved in planning programs to meet the needs and problems of older adults; others are active at the legislative level to help formulate a response to this population shift. Those workers at the direct service level are interacting increasingly with older people, who are both individual clients and parts of their families' problems and solutions.

The past several decades have been a period of rapid development in family therapy as a *bona fide* method of clinical practice. However, there has been a dearth of applications of this modality to the elderly. What has existed has typically focused upon family issues relating to the placement of the elder in a nursing home. An exception is the book by Herr and Weakland (1979) in which these authors broached the subject from the reference point of "applied gerontology." Then in 1989, Hughston, Christopherson, and Bonjean edited a collection of articles on psychotherapy for older adults and their families. This work is a handbook designed to incorporate recent understandings of both aging and family therapy, with the intent of introducing family therapy and practice into the practice of gerontology.

We do not propose to present all aspects of gerontology. The emphasis instead is upon the selection of factors relevant to family intervention in order to illustrate principles of family therapy and their application to work with older adults. Specific tools are presented for the assessment of the elderly and their families. Components of treatment are discussed. Certain issues commonly related to aging serve as the context for the involvement of families in the treatment of their elder members. And implications for policy and program stress the need to incorporate the family into planning for aspects of aging in our society.

Models of family therapy that have developed to address the problems of younger generations are appropriate for clinical work with older adults. Although several forms of family therapy are recognized, we find that no one modality in itself is sufficient for working with this age group. Thus we draw upon several for concepts as well as for strategies and techniques of practice. In so doing, we do not claim to have integrated the different approaches but rather to have selected from among them those ideas that are especially relevant and helpful in understanding and facilitating change in older adults and their families. And finally our family-centered model represents what we consider to be good social work practice with any age group.

This book focuses upon guidelines for the assessment and treatment of older adults in the context of their families. Assessment and intervention take into account a variety of levels of interaction, several views of the family process, and specific points of family conflict that create potential for change. The following chapters describe and illustrate in greater detail the methods specific to these factors. First we define and then explore in depth the eco-systemic approach to addressing the needs of older adults and their families. In Chapter 2 we concentrate on defining the problem and engaging the family, both when the elder member of the family is the one referred for treatment and when the problem is evidenced by another family member. In Chapter 3 we delineate some techniques of assessment in relation to a framework for understanding the problems of the elderly and their families. This serves as the foundation for change. Chapter 4 presents some tools for family treatment and explores the special situations of ethnicity, gender, and culture as they apply to family therapy with the elderly. Chapter 5 focuses on common issues of aging that are related to the life cycle, including salient features of recent changes in family structure within our society. Case illustrations demonstrate the importance of family involvement in the treatment of problems related to aging. In Chapter 6 we discuss family involvement in the treatment of problems not usually considered to be part of normal aging but nevertheless experienced by a significant number of older adults and their families. Finally, some implications for policy and program planning and for the training of human service providers are outlined in Chapter 7 to support the development of family-centered work with older adults. A glossary of some terms commonly used in the field of family therapy and a reference list conclude the book.

For in-depth presentations of family-centered practice based on systems theory, the reader is referred to Hartman and Laird (1983), Hoffman (1981), and Walsh (1982). An account of the specific modalities of family therapy may be obtained from the writings of Salvador Minuchin (1974, 1978, 1981) for the presentation of the structural approach; from Mara Selvini Palazzoli (1978), Lynn Hoffman (1981), and Peggy Papp (1983) for the strategic approach; from Murray Bowen (1978) and Jeannette Kramer (1985) for the intergenerational approach; and from Paul Watzlawick (1967, 1974), Virginia Satir (1967), and Richard Bandler and John Grinder (1975, 1976) for the communications approach. Although the different approaches to family systems work stem from contributions by several significant authors, those we have cited will give a basic view of each modality.

We have found upon consultation with human service providers in the field that frequently, although highly committed to helping the elderly and their families, workers are hampered by a lack of information necessary to achieve this goal. We hope that this handbook will provide some assistance to these dedicated and vital professionals.

Chapter 1

A SYSTEMIC VIEW OF OLDER ADULTS AND THEIR FAMILIES

This chapter provides a theoretical framework for understanding the elderly and their problems within the context of their families. Using a case illustration, we relate family issues to an eco-systemic perspective as well as to the family life cycle. Several concepts central to family assessment and treatment are then presented in association with the stage in the life cycle of the family. These concepts include the constructs of boundary, role flexibility, congruent communication, and goodness-of-fit. We conclude the chapter with an introductory view of the family in its transactions with society and its organizational caregivers.

THINKING FAMILY

A multigenerational, family-focused frame of reference, that is, "thinking family," should guide social work at all levels of assessment and intervention. This emphasis upon family is not meant to deny the many alienated, lonely, troubled, and needy elderly. Instead it underscores our belief that the older adult's life, problems, and needs should be viewed in the context of family.

The increase in the number of older people means more four- and five-generation families exist today, with a rising percentage of older adults aged 85 and over occurring in the population (Butler & Lewis,

1982). Moreover considerable evidence supports the notions that older adults maintain strong family ties and that the family is the major caregiver for those elders needing assistance (Moroney, 1980, pp. 29-34). Older people are for the most part active members of multigenerational families, sometimes providing rich resources to them and sometimes contributing to intergenerational conflict. They are thus involved with other generations in an important and influential relationship.

The following case example illustrates the importance of "thinking family" when providing assistance to older adults.

THE BERRY FAMILY

The Berry family is a middle-class family living in a small city in the Midwest. The Berrys consist of Steven, age 38, his sister Barbara, age 27, another sister living out of state, and their parents, John and Martha, ages 70 and 68 respectively.

Steven contacted a family agency to request help for his mother who had threatened suicide. This information had come to Steven the night before in a phone call from his father, who was in panic. According to the father, Steven's mother had been drinking, had become argumentative and depressed, and had run out of the home and disappeared. She was found several hours later, sitting on the steps of a house nearby and talking to neighbors about not wanting to live any longer. Steven revealed too that he had recently begun to have serious concerns about both of his parents. He and his sister Barbara had received frequent phone calls over the past several months from one or the other of their parents, who complained of terrible, sometimes violent arguments. John Berry had moved out of the house once before and was threatening to do so again. He had spoken to Steven previously about his concern over Martha's drinking and depression.

Steven had talked with Barbara and his other sister. They agreed that he should seek help for their mother. He said all siblings were becoming increasingly anxious about the marriage and the welfare of their parents. Steven in particular was feeling caught in the middle of the parental conflict because he was the one most called on for help and advice. He was feeling confused, anxious, and helpless in this unfamiliar role of counselor to his parents. He hoped his mother could be seen immediately. As it happened, the practitioner he contacted was a family therapist who invited both parents and the son and daughter to the first session. The second daughter was unable to attend the meeting but was informed about what took place later.

The first meeting started with an investigation of the precipitating event. What emerged was the picture of a new pattern. The couple had a long-established ritual of a cocktail hour before dinner, which in the last several months had expanded to include drinking after dinner. As the evening progressed, they would begin to talk of old grievances, usually initiated by Martha. Arguing would ensue and escalate, and sometimes become out of control. John thought Martha was depressed about life in general and he worried about the risk of her suicide. Martha recognized that she had become increasingly angry with him recently but denied thinking about suicide. Both attributed the arguments to their use of alcohol but thought there were other problems too.

As the first session proceeded, what evolved was the following picture of the family and their worries. John and Martha had been married for 40 years. He had been a high school English and drama teacher until his retirement 5 years previously. She had never worked outside the home, although she had always dreamed of being a fashion designer. While the couple had experienced problems in their marriage for the past 15 years, these did not become acute until John's retirement.

Each blamed the other for the difficulties. John complained that his wife could not give up past resentments and held grudges against him for things he claimed to have long since forgotten. He believed that she held him responsible for the frustration of never having had the career that she wanted. He also commented that she had never been the same since an "ill-advised" hysterectomy in her 50s, followed by what she now regarded as harmful psychiatric treatment. He said she blamed him for agreeing to both interventions.

Martha stated that her life had been upset ever since John retired. As she put it, "He retired, I didn't." Before his retirement, John taught and directed student plays, and now he made Martha his audience and "lectured" her. She complained that she no longer had time for her reading and art projects because of his demands on her time. She listed all of the ways in which she had had to shift her life to accommodate to his new time frame and schedule. She felt he was invading her domain and getting in her way even though he might believe he was trying to help her. Meanwhile he was feeling rejected and bewildered that his attempts to relieve her of some household chores were perceived in such a way.

Another serious issue between the couple, and one in which their children were also invested, was their decision to winter in Florida. The

family home was in a northern state, and John had insisted that he no
longer wanted to endure the cold weather. Reluctantly Martha had
agreed to purchase a condominium in Florida, but now resented being
taken away from her friends and grandchildren. She felt she had no
choice in the matter and had to play the "good wife" role. All her
children voiced discomfort with the disruption of the family rituals at
Christmas caused by their parents' move; they talked of missing the
family gatherings. Expanding the exploration of family life further, the
therapist discovered that Martha's 88-year-old mother lived in Florida as
did Martha's brother, and there was conflict in those relationships as well.

The drinking behavior of a predinner cocktail had been a contained
ritual for many years with no evidence of loss of control or increased
tolerance on the part of either John or Martha. Martha's mother had
apparently become an alcoholic in her later years, but there was no other
history of substance abuse in either family of origin.

It became clear that the problems that this family was currently
experiencing consisted of stresses of normative life cycle transitions.
These stresses were mixed with issues from the past that had never been
resolved. Being family-oriented, the therapist recognized that the life
transitions that the older adults faced were generating difficulties for
all family members. Each person had been affected as the parents tried
to restructure their lives. The adult children were drawn into the parental conflict in a most uncomfortable way and felt torn between their fear
about the welfare of the parents and their reluctance to take sides. All
members were reacting to the disruption in the usual family rituals and
ways of being together and were experiencing a sense of loss in that
regard. The family therapist recognized too that, as so often happens,
old issues and unresolved grievances were surfacing at the   transition.
Relationship difficulties in the marriage, which had been simmering on
the back burner, were coming to a boil, and something had to be done.
Parent-child problems such as Steven's and Barbara's belief and resentment that their father's work always took precedence over his spending
time with them came to the fore. In addition John and Martha reflected
upon their families of origin and revealed a number of concerns about
relationships with their remaining siblings and other relatives. Martha
of course had some lively issues with her mother in Florida, one of
which was her mother's involvement with a younger man of 78 years.
So what had been presented as a problem with one individual had
expanded to include a network of people and their concerns.

All of the issues identified above were addressed during the course of work with the Berry family. Martha and John were seen together. Therapy focused on changing the dysfunctional patterns that stood in the way of their growth as individuals and as a couple. They were able to develop a new daily predinner ritual that did not include alcohol, and the arguments diminished. They talked openly of old grievances, present dissatisfactions, and their worries and fears about the future. As a result they resolved many misunderstandings and became more tolerant and responsive to each other's needs. John became appreciative of his wife's need for space and time for her own pursuits. He even helped to build some work space for her art projects. Martha began to share more of herself and her time with John. Together they devised a daily sched ule that included some joint endeavors as well as time apart from each other. In other words, they organized new daily rituals that lent stability, order, and satisfaction to their lives. This is a task, sometimes unrecognized as such, that all older couples face when entering retirement.

Another goal of therapy pertained to Martha and John as individuals, even though the changes affected their interaction as a couple. John's teaching life had great meaning for him, and he felt a sense of emptiness and loss of purpose without his work. Moreover his involvement with work had influenced the couple's functioning by regulating their closeness. John and Martha were able to attain a more comfortable intimacy as communication improved, but John was left with the need to feel productive. Connecting him with opportunities to teach on a voluntary basis helped fill this need, as did his idea to form a drama club for older adults in his home in Florida. This also decreased the complaints from Martha about his lecturing her and using her as an audience.

Martha's lack of friends in Florida and her distance from her family during the holiday season troubled her and was an irritant in her relationship with John. As she explored some options in therapy she realized ways in which she could reach out more to develop desired contacts. She accepted an invitation to join a group of her sorority sisters. Her artwork provided avenues for connections. In one session she and John and their children agreed upon a plan to be together at Christmastime. To reach such an agreement John compromised on his position about returning north during the winter. One payoff for him, however, was the relationship achieved with his children as they talked of wanting to be closer to him.

Thus what began as a request for help with one family member enabled the therapist to provide assistance to the entire family as well.

AN ECO-SYSTEMIC PERSPECTIVE

The Berry case example illustrates not only "thinking family" but also the eco-systemic view that underlies the approach presented in this book. By "eco-system" we mean the complex of a human system, in this case a family, and its environment, which function together as a unit in nature. Ecology is defined as the science concerned with the interrelationship of organisms and their environment (*Webster's*, 1977). By system, we are not referring to a social organization, but instead to a "unit containing feedback structure and therefore competent to process information" (Bateson, 1971, p. 243). Keeney (1979, p. 120) conceptualizes a system in terms of the role played by symptoms:

1. Difficulties in any part of the relationship system may give rise to symptomatic expression in other parts of the system.
2. Symptomatic relief at one part of the system may result in a transfer of symptomatic expression to another site.
3. Significant change . . . in any part of the system may result in change in other parts of the system.

Keeney characterized family diagnosis and therapy as "an expanding view of the identified patient's relational field—from partial families to whole families, intergenerational families, and extended networks" (1979, p. 125). Individuals and their problems can best be understood and changed in the context of the person's total ecology, that is, the persons's environment and human network. In reference to work with older adults, Hartman and Laird have pointed out that "the unit of attention is the ecological system which includes the aging person, his or her current family system, the physical, social, and cultural environment, and the intergenerational family system" (1983, p. 359). Elsewhere they illustrate the metaphor of ecology in terms of

focusing on the interface between families and the larger environment. . . . The primary mission of the family-centered practitioner, then, is the enhancement of the quality of life, of that delicate, adaptive balance between human beings and their ecological environments. This enhancement may well come about through change in individual or family functioning, in the larger systems on which the family depends for nurturance or growth, or in the transactions among these systems. (1983, p. 6)

Our case example of the Berry family illustrates several ecological principles. First of all, the focus was not just on an individual. The therapist addressed Martha's difficulties in relation to her network of relationships. Although Martha was presented by her family as the target for change, the therapist asked her extended family to attend both the initial interview and most subsequent ones. And even in the absence of other family members, the effect of others was part of the focus.

Second, Martha and her behavior were not viewed in terms of pathology. Instead her behavior was considered in relation to its context, specifically the life cycle stage of retirement as well as the human interrelationships that were involved. The assessment thus broadened the picture to include the family and the ecology of the problem.

Treatment itself included reframing or redefining Martha's and John's difficulties in terms of normative life transitions, with an emphasis upon resources. Reallocation and negotiation of roles, rituals, and activities occurred both within the larger family and also for its individuals in relation to the community. Martha and John were helped to find new predinner customs as a vehicle for their intimacy and communication. John obtained role satisfaction from teaching in the community, which allowed the couple the space to reestablish a mutual level of sharing. And the extended family negotiated times of reunion as well as responsibilities for assisting the parents.

In accordance with another principle of family-centered and ecosystemic practice, the therapist clearly addressed the family as multigenerational. The frame of reference was widened to include Martha's mother and their relationship as well as John's and Martha's relationships with their children.

Thus problem-solving skills and resources were activated in many areas. The Berrys built a more viable and effective network both within their family and in its relation to the larger community. What was presented initially as Martha's problem, or perhaps Martha's and John's, came to be viewed in a much wider context, that of the family in its entirety and as a system.

LIFE STAGE ISSUES

As was clear in the above case example, the later life stages of an individual are also family life stages; many generations are both active in and affected by the transition of the elderly family members. Where problems, needs, and developmental issues surface is at the interface of the older and younger generations.

Carter and McGoldrick (1980, p. 17) delineate the emotional transition of the later life stage of the nuclear family as comprising the acceptance of the shifting of generational roles. The following are developmental changes needed to facilitate this task:

1. Maintaining own and/or couple functioning and interests in face of physiological decline; exploration of new familial and social role options.
2. Support for a more central role for middle generation.
3. Making room in the system for the wisdom and experience of the elderly; supporting the older generation without overfunctioning for them.
4. Dealing with loss of spouse, siblings, and other peers and preparation for own death. Life review and integration.

Further, Carter and McGoldrick identify substages in this life cycle as follows: launching or setting the stage, retirement, grandparenthood, widow(er)hood, illness and dependency, and eventual death (1980, pp. 198-210).

The vignette of the Berry family demonstrates several issues common in families at the later stage of their life cycle. The Berrys were struggling with factors of renegotiation of marital roles at the time of retirement, geographical relocation, adjustment of rituals for maintaining both marital and intergenerational connections, and unresolved issues from the past that were activated by current situations. The Berrys had clearly been blocked in the "exploration of new familial and social roles." Carter and McGoldrick (1980) refer to the primary task for a couple at the husband's retirement as "his incorporation within the home" (p. 201). John's recent retirement was a major transition to which he and his family had failed to adjust. Treatment of the Berry family included addressing John and Mary's marital roles as well as John's need for meaningful productivity.

Carter and McGoldrick point as well to the common practice of change of residence as a source of dislocation and loss of connectedness with family, neighbors, and community. The therapist enabled this family to communicate and problem solve about such issues more effectively. Unresolved previous resentments were raised that cleared the way to maintain connectedness with all three generations. The son's relationship with his father and Martha's with her elderly mother became points of focus.

The impact of this family's failure to negotiate the earlier "empty nest" transition was now interfering with its ability to handle the later life stage of retirement. This last factor relates to the stresses of the *sandwich generation*. The term refers to the modern-day phenomenon of four- and five-generation families in which the older adults have parents who increasingly require attention just when the middle generation expects freedom from caretaking because their own children are grown. The Berrys' therapist helped Steven and his sisters adapt to their growing roles of assisting their parents while also managing their own responsibilities. And, of course, late-life-onset or chronic alcoholism is an all too frequent occurrence that compels immediate attention. Several of these issues are discussed further in Chapters 5 and 6.

CONCEPTS OF FAMILY-CENTERED PRACTICE

In the assessment and treatment of families at the later life stage, human service providers should have an understanding of central concepts of family practice. In line with that goal, we have identified several constructs that we deem to be of particular relevance for work with this population. Drawing upon the approach of family-centered social work practice as developed by Hartman and Laird (1983), we have selected for emphasis the concepts of boundary, hierarchy, role flexibility, congruent communication, and goodness-of-fit. Each is defined at the point of discussion.

Boundary

A system's boundary consists of that which distinguishes what is within a system from what is outside it. Boundaries function to protect the differentiation or delineation of a system, whether the system be a family, one of its members, an organization, or a larger society. Boundaries are characterized by the continuum of enmeshment to disengagement, that is, from one pole of family members' overinvolvement with each other to the opposite extreme of alienation and lack of connection with one another.

Modern-day living involves "growing isolation, unavailability of resources, and the diminution of meaningful exchanges with the environment . . . as people age" (Hartman & Laird, 1983, p. 359). It is at the boundaries between the older adult and the environment that much of the work with the elderly occurs. Boundaries of families in late life stages illustrate the degree of social isolation surrounding the elder and how connected the older adult is to the family and the family to community resources. The potential move of John and Martha Berry stemmed from and highlighted their issues of social isolation and connectedness.

How boundary lines are drawn around the elderly is a frequent cause of conflict and dysfunction and is a systemic issue. Intrusive adult children or bossy elders, each fearful of being neglected or losing power, exhibit boundary issues. When working with older adults and their families, boundaries may need to be renegotiated between the elder and the middle generation. The goal of this task is to bring closure to previously unresolved conflicts or to address emergent ones created by the aging of the family members. Treatment of boundary issues might focus upon situations of adult children infantilizing or ignoring an elder (disengagement), or minimizing an elder's needs or crisis (disengagement), or seeking to merge emotionally with the older parent (enmeshment).

Hierarchy

Another central concept is *hierarchy*. This term in family therapy refers to the organization of a family's several generations, each holding a different level of status and power. Hierarchy is related to boundaries, in that subsystems such as the spouse subsystem "must establish a boundary to protect it from interference by demands and needs of others, such as . . . members of the extended family" (Hartman & Laird, 1983, p. 83). Dysfunctional patterns can emerge when the family's hierarchy is not clear or has become fixed in roles, rules, and structures of power at an earlier stage in the life cycle. It is not unusual for an elder in these circumstances to address an adult child as though he or she were a youth, thus alienating or disempowering the middle-aged member. In the Berry case, Steven and Barbara were experiencing a pull to parent the older generation and were unsure how to respond.

Family theorists have suggested that confused hierarchy produces emotional and/or behavioral symptoms in family members (Minuchin, 1974; Minuchin, Rosman, & Baker, 1978; Minuchin & Fishman, 1981; Haley, 1983). Martha Berry's conflictual and distanced relationship with her mother implies the presence of hierarchical issues in Martha's own family of origin.

Role Flexibility

The presence of a variety of adaptive responses, known as *role flexibility*, has been correlated with successful aging. Role flexibility of family members enables them to share and reassign tasks and responses to developmental needs as well as to emergencies or "geriatric crises." Such a family system will support the later life adjustment of the older adult as well. This in turn predicts longevity in addition to satisfaction in old age (Carter & McGoldrick, 1980).

There were many examples in the Berry family of role problems: Martha's resentment over her mother's "young" husband, Steven and Barbara's resistance to a view of their parents that included the parental needs, and of course John's adjustment to the role of retiree and Martha's entrenchment in the role of "good wife."

Congruent Communication

The need for verbal and nonverbal messages to be consistent with one another is what is meant by *congruent communication*. This need is heightened dramatically for the elderly, who usually experience a reduction in the sharpness of one or more of their five senses as part of normal aging. Bandler and Grinder (1976) postulate that the process of communication takes place through what they term "channels of communication." These channels are either visual, auditory, or kinesthetic involving touch. When an older adult experiences a reduction in one or more of the senses, access to the channels of communication is thus limited. The remaining channels then become especially crucial, both for communication of mutual needs and for assessment of reality.

Goodness-of-Fit

As conceptualized by Germain and Gitterman (1980), *goodness-of-fit* refers to the need for individuals and primary groups to be in a supportive relationship with their physical and social environments and with the political and economic structures of society. These relationships are conducive to the continual experience of "environmental challenges, opportunities, and obstacles to adaptive functioning. Some of these upset the goodness-of-fit and lead to undesirable or unmanageable stress" (1980, p. 137). A goodness-of-fit is deemed essential for adaptation and growth. The theorists speak of adaptation as the result of a "joint achievement of individual and environment in reaching a goodness-of-fit between adaptive skills and qualities, the progressive forces in the person, and growth-supporting properties and structures of the environment" (Germain & Gitterman, 1980, p. 80). This model is compatible with that of Erikson's (1950) life stages, in which an uncompleted task of one stage becomes a residue that hinders the mastery of subsequent stages.

We saw examples of such barriers to development in the Berry family. Unfinished adaptation at the stage of retirement, and possibly earlier at the time of the children leaving home, was interfering with present-day functioning. John's lost connection to his support network in the community had not been replaced. He exhibited stress from blocked productivity and support. Similarly Martha's relationship with her primary environment, her home, became stressful to her when John's attempts to be helpful usurped her roles.

The above concepts from family systems theory not only stand alone in their relevance, but also hold significant meaning for the tasks of the family in its late life cycle. Each of the life cycle phases is a point of heightened potential for individual and/or family dysfunction in relation to the above concepts, as the life cycle tasks define so many problems in terms of the concepts. Not only should the human service provider be knowledgeable about family systems, but also that theory should be juxtaposed with the assessment of the family's position in time.

A TRANSACTIONAL VIEW

The family should be viewed as positioned relative to the larger societal system. The extensive eco-system as it affects the family, with potential for providing support and nurture, is an integral aspect of family functioning. How the family seeks and accepts help defines the extent of the resourcefulness of members of the middle or sandwich generation, who are instrumental in family cohesion and who perform as the major caretakers of older members.

The family's ability to change will also reflect its goodness-of-fit with the community's human service network. The transactional view therefore needs to encompass an examination of the role of human service caregivers from the community. When in a functional network, these providers can in themselves effect dramatic change. But when their work is embedded in a dysfunctional system, perhaps exhibiting its own inappropriate boundaries or unclear communication, the caregivers' potential for assistance to families in need is limited. This important topic is addressed more fully in the last chapter.

SUMMARY

We have presented a theoretical framework for understanding the elderly and their problems that is based upon "thinking family." The importance of an eco-systemic view has been stressed. We related the life cycle to the process of aging and explored implications for the older adult and the family. Concepts that are fundamental to the practice of family therapy have been discussed and applied to treatment of families with older members. Finally we have drawn attention to societal aspects of our approach to clinical work with issues of aging.

Now let us proceed to the clinical process itself. The practitioner's understanding of change and the means by which the clinician approaches the task of effecting change are components crucial to the success of treatment.

Chapter 2

SETTING THE STAGE

The focus of this chapter is on the clinical view that should be taken by the human service provider in order to effect change in the family system and its members. This approach begins with reframing the problem from one that is linear to a systemic one; that is, from the problem of an individual to the problem of the family as a system in itself and within larger systems. The problem must also be presented to the clients as solvable, thus releasing them from their more limited views or "frames" so that they can obtain new, freeing views that allow positive change. This skill includes "joining" with family members. The clinician should also be adept at recognizing obstacles to bringing people together, including myths of aging, or "ageism," which may be operative. The practitioner in addition should be alert to the possibility of the presenting problem masking an issue related to the older generation, even when the presenting problem is attributed to another family member. Finally, a decision must be made as to who is to be included in the family sessions.

THE SYSTEMIC VIEW OF CHANGE

A practitioner with a linear view of change perceives clinical processes in terms of cause and effect. The focus is on the individual. What was the origin of that person's problem? When did it begin? What or who made it happen? What is the pathology of the person in question?

Psychiatric nomenclature and the traditional medical model are the foundation of the anticontextual approach: "The individual therapist tells the patient: 'Change yourself. Work with yourself so you will grow. Look inside and change what you find there.' " (Minuchin & Fishman, 1981, p. 197).

The systemic view, on the other hand, emphasizes ecology, relationship, and whole systems. Core elements include interrelationship, complexity, and context. The systemic view is based upon the concept of homeostasis. In a homeostatic system, the behavior of one family member is felt and responded to by other members in such a way that the operation of the system is homeostatic, or self-maintaining. Behavior remains within the limits of flexibility allowed by the family. The family therapist thus asks for details, not of the individual with the problem, but instead of "the family dance." Who does what? Who responds next, and how? What function does a problematic behavior have in the family process? How does the behavior promote family stability or predictability? How much flexibility does the system allow and how do family members maintain these limits? In the case illustration in Chapter 1, the focus was not on Martha, the individual. Instead the therapist in that case explored her husband's recent retirement and the resulting ripples throughout the family as other members attempted to regain family stability.

Systemic approaches thus utilize a frame of reference of "thinking family" in which the family is understood to be a system. One feature of a system is that its various parts exist as a whole that is greater than the sum of its parts; that is, the family processes have qualities of their own and exist in addition to the processes of individual members. Not only did Steven Berry have an identity as an individual, but he also experienced himself as "one of the Berrys" with family expectations of being loving, loyal, hard working, and responsible. He responded accordingly to his parents' pleas for assistance.

The systemic view also encompasses an intergenerational perspective. The family is a system that exists in time. The norms, roles, and expectations of its members are passed down through generations. They are especially evident at transitions. Steven Berry was uncomfortable when he felt thrust into the role of caretaker or mediator, a role his family had always ascribed to adult female members. And his parents' forthcoming move was unearthing buried issues of conflict between Martha and her mother.

Not only do families exist as a system in time; they also operate on a horizontal axis. Families cannot escape the current pressures of the community within which they live. It was not just the norms of his family that Steven was experiencing as a source of conflict, but also those of the larger traditional society. The Berrys were reflecting our modern world's changes in mobility and patterns of retirement. They may need help finding that goodness-of-fit that supports family members' needs within the larger societal context at a particular point in time.

A SOLVABLE PROBLEM, OR REFRAMING THE PROBLEM

Haley (1976) states that "the way one labels a human dilemma can crystallize a problem and make it chronic" (p. 3). He goes on to say that "if therapy is to end properly, it must begin properly—by negotiating a solvable problem and discovering the social situation that makes the problem necessary. The act of therapy begins with the way the problem is examined" (p. 9).

The clinician, prepared with a systemic view of problems and their resolution, forms in interpersonal terms a hypothesis of the presenting problem from the information initially presented by the referral source. The "symptom" is understood to be a message in an interconnected relationship network having properties of feedback. The hypothesis regarding the present problem and its resolution must then be tested during the assessment phase. This process leads to reframing or restating the problem in terms that make it solvable.

Minuchin and Fishman describe the process this way:

> The therapist's first problem in joining the family is to define the therapeutic reality. Therapy is a goal-oriented enterprise, to which not all truths are relevant. By observing the family members' transactions in the therapeutic system, the therapist selects the data that will facilitate problem solving.
>
> Therapy starts, therefore, with the clash between two framings of reality. The family's framing is relevant for the continuity and maintenance of the organism more or less as it is; the therapeutic framing is related to the goal of moving the family toward a more differentiated and competent dealing with their dysfunctional reality. (1981, p. 74)

Walsh (1982) points to the difference between coping or dysfunction as being related to the family's explanation of the life event or situation in order to make sense of what happened, why it happened, and what will resolve it. Reframing targets these factors.

In the illustration of the Berry family, the family's view of the presenting problem of Martha's suicidal threats was widened to include the context of the situation: her family and their responses to the recent retirement of John, her husband. The problem was thus reframed in terms of adjustments required at the normal life stage of retirement, goals within family members' reach. Hartman and Laird (1983) provide a typology of reframing and describe this form as one that expands the meaning of a problem. Another type of reframing identified by the above authors is that which alters the view of the purpose of behavior. The presenting problem of an anxious and overburdened husband who resentfully takes care of his low-functioning wife can also be framed in terms of the wife's depression providing him with a way to feel needed and important. This new perspective allows the problem to be defined as purposeful and mutually maintained, and makes available more possibilities for intervention.

A third form of reframing, according to Hartman and Laird, is the presentation of the problem as a solution to another problem. The following is an illustration from practice:

> A grandfather had moved near his adult children and, long after getting settled, was producing problems for them to solve. Assessment revealed that he was creating or not solving problems in order to maintain contact with his adult children. The faster they resolved the problems, the faster he presented them, with little energy remaining for positive interactions. This cycle, rapidly bringing the family to a rupture between the generations, was successfully reversed in treatment as the family was helped to address its members' anxieties at the level of relationships. The grandfather's problems were alleviated.

No matter what the problem and its context, how a problem is reframed is crucial to the process and success of treatment. And the reframing must render the problem solvable. O'Connor (1989, p. 72) succinctly points out that "reality depends upon our perception of it and a simple change in one's point of view can lead to innumerable new possibilities." Clinicians have a responsibility to help clients think in a new way so they may become unstuck from their views, or frames, and develop new ones with potential for positive change.

The application of reframing is related to the framework for understanding change presented by Watzlawick, Weakland, and Fisch (1974, p. 10). Their model classifies first-order change as "one that occurs within a given system which itself remains unchanged," and second-order change as "one whose occurrence changes the system itself." When the family's course of treatment involves primarily first-order change, a minimum of reframing may be needed. For example, adult children of a recently invalided older parent willingly follow the suggestion to obtain assistance from community services such as Meals on Wheels and thus reduce their own burden and feelings of resentment. On the other hand a family whose treatment necessitates second-order change would resist such advice. Their problem should instead be reframed in a way that moves them to a workable solution. For instance, their resistance to obtaining help might be presented as serving to protect them from facing and resolving earlier resentments or guilt toward their aging parent.

Another way of conceptualizing reframing is as a process. Herr and Weakland depict reframing as consisting of two steps:

> The first is to determine in your own mind what new approaches the family needs to take to reach their mutually agreed-upon goal. Such a determination is usually based on your professional experience. . . . Knowing what your clients should do differently is the easier part. The second, more difficult aspect of reframing is to suggest effectively how the problem might be handled differently—in your client's language. (1979, p. 143)

Thus an important element of presenting the problem as solvable includes its statement in the client's own words. This "simple reframing" serves to communicate the clinician's ideas in the clients' language. A more complex reframing can be accomplished in terms of a metaphor for the family problem or dynamics, but again in the language of the clients' world. In workshops for professionals, Minuchin has used the metaphor of a "finely tuned Swiss watch" to interpret to a family the interrelationships of its members' behaviors. Particular interests of the family, a member's occupation, shared experiences—such focal points in the family's life can be used as a unifying theme for goal attainment and, when stated in familiar words, may enhance the family members' readiness to make positive change.

Reframing, when thought of as a means to convey a message from the therapist to the client in the client's language, is also a means of "joining" with the family members.

JOINING: ENGAGING THE FAMILY

As defined by Minuchin and Fishman (1981), joining is "letting the family know that the therapist understands them and is working with and for them" (pp. 31-32). It is

> more an attitude than a technique, and it is the umbrella under which all therapeutic transactions occur. . . . Only under (the therapist's) protection can the family have the security to explore alternatives, try the unusual, and change. Joining is the glue that holds the therapeutic system together.

Joining first comes into play at the initial contact with the family and any of its members. The clinician consciously identifies points of similarity with the family. An older therapist might share with an elder client a mutual understanding of the need to walk gingerly up the clinic's sidewalk in icy weather. A clinician with children could speak sympathetically to young parents trying to keep their youngsters from interrupting or "bothering" the grandparent. The practitioner might comment empathetically to family members about how difficult it is to find the clinic.

Tone of voice and speed of speech should be geared deliberately to match those of the family. Vocabulary too needs to be appropriate to the situation and the person. For instance, a blue-collar family with no prior experience with counseling might feel intimidated by a worker using psychological terms. An older adult may respond best to terms of respect suitable to the person's age and status. Sensitivity to an elder's cultural background and to the stigma often connected with therapy years ago may lead the clinician to speak of "talking about" the subject instead of referring to "counseling" or "therapy."

Other forms of joining include sharing one's own feelings, such as some uneasiness about being a stranger when the family members all know each other. This may give permission to the family to share their feelings as well. Too, the approach of clearly restating the problem as a family problem with everyone involved in the resolution is a form of joining that can also go far toward facilitating the participation of other family members. If an elder rambles in telling her history in a way some of the family find tedious, her presentation can be taped and then played to the family, who can "fast-forward" through repetitions, a strategy that validates needs of the various members without excluding input from the elder. Home visits are helpful in easing the transition to sessions in the office, and in cases of older adults' immobility, home may be the only suitable site. There the worker meets the family on its own turf. This is less threatening to hesitant members and is simultaneously a rich source for assessment. Assessment strategies often double as means of engagement into therapy, or joining; they are explored further in Chapter 3.

Joining is not only a process for the beginning of therapy, but also continues throughout its duration:

> The worker demonstrates an understanding and appreciation of the family, sensitivity to their dilemmas, and respect for the family's coherence and their efforts to survive. The worker's joining stance serves to validate and confirm both the individuals in the family and the system as a whole. (Hartman & Laird, 1983, p. 146)

A good rule of thumb for the clinician who feels "stuck" in facilitating change is to ask: Do I need to join with the family?

Joining with the family members is the foundation for the application of concepts such as reframing, and even for treatment itself. It is the crux of engaging a family for treatment.

OBSTACLES TO ENGAGING THE FAMILY

Obstacles to family-centered work with the elderly can arise from within society, from the elderly, from family members of any generation, and from clinicians themselves. Practitioners should be aware of these obstacles in order to intervene appropriately with families.

Myths About Aging

A reluctance or resistance to engaging the elderly in treatment is fostered by various societal myths. Ageism is a prevailing myth regarding the elderly and the process of aging. It relegates older adults to a hopeless status that predicts the impossibility of change, a uniformity of elders and their problems, and an inevitable decline. Reality indicates, however, that people's individuality increases with age. Moreover much of what has been labeled "senility" is reversible when depression, use of medication, and metabolic or infectious disorders are assessed and treated (Butler & Lewis, 1982). See also Chapter 6.

Another myth contends that elders are abandoned by their families. This belief is countered by the finding that the majority of older adults live with other family members and that over 80% live within an hour of at least one child (Walsh, 1982). In addition, families are the source of approximately 80% of all home health care (Nelson, 1982). Institutions are a last resort, with only 5% of the elderly in institutions at any one time (Butler & Lewis, 1982). The average age at admission is 80 (Walsh, 1982).

Societal myths stem from a lack of knowledge about the aging process. They also reflect a prejudicial attempt to avoid responsibility to the aging while denying one's own mortality. Societal myths of aging are often supported by family attitudes.

Resistance by the Elderly

Elders themselves may be the seat of resistance to family treatment that would involve them. They likely were born in an era when mental illness was equated with "being crazy," assistance or treatment entailed only custodial care, and entering a psychiatric institution might well be for life. The stigma of mental illness was paramount. Even if older adults are informed about psychology, in their early years the mode of treatment was almost exclusively that of individual therapy, and the concept of family treatment may be unfamiliar to them.

The elderly are the "new poor" who, unless wealthy at the time of retirement, may not be able to afford treatment. The threat of future limitations to Social Security and Medicare benefits enhance the likeliness of this barrier. Finally the elders' own attitudes may discourage a consideration of the utilization of family treatment. Their statements might sound like: "I do not want to interfere in my children's lives," "I have lived my life and am too old to change," or "That [issue, situation] is over, why bring up the past?" Yet if the elder is present at family sessions, infantilization and denial of the elder's strengths are less likely to occur, and the family is enriched.

Resistance by Family Members

Obstacles to a family-focused approach to treating the elderly may originate within other generations. Middle-aged adults, who readily bring their children to treatment because the children are viewed as less powerful, may nevertheless hesitate to involve directly their own parents. The unspoken fear of being cast in the role of child in the presence of the elder parent reflects an issue relating to the hierarchy of authority, with underlying fears of being undermined or of secrets being revealed. Avoidant attitudes expressed by the middle generation include: "Mother is too old, senile, sick to be involved," "Any stress will bring her closer to death," "Mother is not really a part of this, she does not live with us." In this case, Mother's isolation, even in death, is more bearable to the family than her possible "upset" and its ramifications.

The youngest generation may express resistance to family treatment of the elderly, with attitudes attempting to relegate the grandparents to obsolescence: "Grandparents are 'out of it' "; "Things are different now." These attitudes may mask the children's fear of being outnumbered if the treatment includes grandparents, especially if the grandparents are perceived as needy and in competition with the children for the attention of the middle generation. Or the grandchildren may fear that more objective grandparents will interfere with the children's blaming of their own parents. In that case the children might attempt to divide and conquer the two adult generations. Similarly an acting-out teenager might seek to blame the parents rather than acknowledge a collusion with the grandparents that serves to sabotage the parental authority. Conversely parents might themselves more readily focus on and thus even foster their child's misbehavior as a distraction from their intergenerational conflicts with their own parents, the grandparents. And, of course, a family's perception of the impact of an event on its various members, including its older adults, is both a source of and a response to resistance by the family to involvement in therapy with the elderly.

Resistance by Clinicians

One possible locus of resistance to the utilization of family approaches for treatment of the elderly may reside in the clinician. Clinical training programs usually offer their students modules focused upon child development, but familiarity with aspects of aging and the families of the elderly are often deemed less crucial for inclusion in the curriculum. And of course the history of the development of family therapy demonstrates that the spotlight has been upon parents and their children. Thus family therapists may exhibit a bias toward child-centered family therapy and invite to sessions only members of the nuclear family. Resistance may also arise from issues potentially inherent in any treatment of the elderly. One form is the view that the elder will die soon and thus does not warrant much effort. The older adult all too frequently is perceived as being resistant to change or even being untreatable. The label of senility renders the elder inaccessible, less than individual, and hopeless.

On the other hand, perhaps the clinician is reluctant to face his or her own mortality. Especially pertinent are the possibilities that the issues relating to the clinician's own parents have not been resolved and that the human service provider may wish to avoid possible feelings of intimidation by the elder client's wisdom or age. Because the life cycle of the older adult is outside the direct personal experience of many workers, their familiarity with issues of aging likely stems from their experience with the lives of their own parents and other family members of older generations, with feelings derived accordingly from these relationships.

The 1971 report of the Committee on Aging of the Group for the Advancement of Psychiatry listed the following reasons for adverse views of staff toward treatment of the elderly (Sprung, 1989):

1. The aged stimulate the therapist's fears about his or her own aging.
2. They arouse the therapist's conflicts about his or her relationship with parental figures.
3. The therapist believes he or she has nothing useful to offer old people, because he or she believes they cannot change their behavior or that their problems are all due to untreatable organic brain disease.
4. The therapist believes that his or her psychodynamic skills will be wasted working with the aged because they are near death and not really deserving of attention.
5. The patient might die while in treatment, which might challenge the therapist's sense of importance.
6. The therapist's colleagues may be contemptuous of his or her efforts on behalf of aged patients. (p. 598)

Human service providers should be encouraged to examine their own attitudes about aging and death and to resolve issues with the aging or deceased members of their own families. Clinicians thus can become more available to older clients and their families with minimal over-involvement, detachment, or burnout. "Realistic" responses to the elderly and their families need to be examined closely as well for societal myths and stereotypes that serve to distance younger workers from their own eventual aging, physical deterioration, and death. Finally, clinicians should be aware of the risk of helping clients live longer than they wish or in a manner that they find abhorrent if the clinicians themselves have not completed their own grief work and faced their own feelings and fears.

Organizational Resistances

Obstacles to family therapy involving the elderly include organizational resistance. The home visits that often are indicated for the less-mobile elderly are frequently not reimbursable for third-party payment and are a relatively expensive use of clinical time. Home visits may be judged by social agency administrators as impractical programming, especially at a time of tight budgetary constraints that result in a limitation of services.

A promising note is the growing trend toward providing family treatment in nursing homes and hospitals, both to facilitate satisfactory adjustment of the elder to the new location as well as to shorten the length of residential care with the goal of returning home. Butler and Lewis (1982, p. xiv), in discussing the delivery of mental health services, state: "The community mental health movement has yet to demonstrate any real commitment to the mental health care of the old," a sad commentary even if partially true, and unfortunately still valid in the last decade of the century.

ISSUES MASKING THE NEED FOR FAMILY THERAPY

The above presentation of obstacles to engaging families for treatment also indicates some of the factors that must be kept in mind when deciding whom to include in treatment. Walsh (1982) clearly states the family systems point of view:

> Clinically, it is rarely the older family members themselves who seek help, although they do suffer from many clinical problems, primary among

which is depression. More often it is members of the next generation who
seek help, and even they often do not present with their problem defined
as relating to a parent. It is often only through careful history taking that
one learns that an aging grandparent is just about to move in or to be taken
to a nursing home, and that the relationship issues around this shift have
been left totally submerged in the family. (p. 187)

Following are some of the issues and problems that may be masked
when a family member seeks treatment, whether the concern is initially
manifested by the elder member or by another family member. An understanding of such issues should help the clinician recognize the need for a
family assessment and a family therapy approach to treatment.

Multiple-Generation Households

We are seeing a greater incidence of more than one generation
sharing a household. This is because of demographic factors such as the
increased life span, the resulting larger percentage of older adults in the
general population, and the higher incidence of four- and five-generation families. Relevant economic factors are nationwide recession, with
increased unemployment and economic hardships.

The result of the higher-density household is that family members
cannot as easily avoid unresolved issues from the past, or the present
realities of the aging process. They are confronted with dilemmas
pertaining to the change in the elder's roles in the family that are
occurring because of aging. Moreover unresolved issues of giving and
receiving may prevent cooperative assumption and redistribution of
duties. It is not infrequent in clinical practice to find an adult who
experienced parental deprivation in childhood now resisting or resent-
ing giving to that parent who has become more needful in later years of
life. Either the withholding, guilty adult or the rejected, depressed elder
may initially seek treatment.

Another form of this dynamic is illustrated by the following case:

Judy K., a married woman in her 40s with a son, age 6 and a daughter, age
2, sought help for emotional exhaustion, headaches, and a concern about
increased conflict between her husband and son. Medical examination
ruled out factors other than indicators of stress, although there was some
concern for her future health if the present level of tension were to
continue. Assessment revealed that Judy's mother, in her late 60s, had a
lifetime stance of invincibility but now was expressing great need in a

struggle against cancer. Judy had never felt loved by her mother and at last was experiencing the appreciation she craved. She was spending long hours at the hospital or at the mother's home between hospitalizations. Judy's previously indulged and newly neglected husband, upon whom demands now fell for child care and household chores, displaced his anger onto his son, because a wife who seemed so noble in her care of the ill was deemed to be beyond reproach.

An early and vital component of treatment was meeting for several family sessions with Judy and her extended family: her father, aunt, uncle, and brother. It was learned that Judy's relatives resented her dominance and were a ready stabilizer for a new pattern of interaction in which assistance to Judy's mother was more equitably distributed. What could have been a continuing support for Judy's dysfunction was thus short-circuited, and Judy then proceeded to grieve her losses more appropriately, with a parallel decrease in strife in her nuclear family.

Family members in close proximity may revive painful, undesired memories of past losses and therefore activate the family's coping methods for handling loss. These coping methods may in themselves precipitate further difficulties, which then become the stated problem at referral.

Changing Family Roles

Changes in roles in the modern family impact the clinical field. The increase in women's participation in the work force may mean that grandparents are asked to raise a second set of children, their grandchildren, and forfeit an expected pleasure from the "spoiling" role of "having all the fun and none of the responsibility." An acceptance of the above requests not only produces a shift in role expectations but also in power assignments. Families with difficulty assigning tasks or with a propensity for dysfunctional communication frequently seek clinical assistance for a problem that stems from this type of breakdown in the system. Conflict can erupt if the grandparents themselves wish to work in later years and refuse or resent the demand for continued parenting. The question of child care and available, appropriate community services becomes highlighted at such a time.

Modern trends of marriage and divorce, with concomitant social manifestations, may be issues for family treatment. The noncustodial parent probably has visitation rights to the children, but this is not necessarily the case for the grandparents, who then experience loss in family support in two dimensions. The divorced adult child likely goes to work; the grandchildren living with the custodial parent may be located at a distance. Chronic illness, which is recognized as a possible effect of divorce (Duffy, Iscoe, & Kurman, 1982), may result in a reduction of the ability of the middle-aged divorced child to care for the older relative and at the same time may increase the demands on the elder. Either the divorced adult or the elder may seek individual treatment for this problem, which is in reality a family systems issue.

Middle Generation Stress

The middle generation has been termed the "buffer generation" or "sandwich generation" (Miller, 1981) in reference to its positioning between a generation that is older and one that is younger. This generation is especially vulnerable to the effects of stress. Children leave but, because of divorce or unemployment, not uncommonly return home with unexpected demands for assistance just as the parents are ready to attend more fully to their own personal needs or careers. Simultaneously the parents' own elder generation is becoming more needful. The middle generation is expected to give financial and emotional aid to their children and even to the grandchildren, but are also the primary caretakers of their own increasingly impaired, elderly parents. And the grandparents may also be providing assistance to their own parents, the great-grandparents and fourth generation.

Care of the frail elderly readily produces stress for the middle generation by restricting its freedom and independence. These caretakers may be isolated from their own support systems within the extended family or the community at large. Financial strain and a deficit of emotional support can be responsible for anxiety and depression among the buffer generation, which functions as a key force in the cohesiveness of the family system.

Intergenerational Conflict

Problems of leaving home are one manifestation of intergenerational conflict (Haley, 1980). As teenagers approach the age for leaving home, parents with a strong need to nurture may infantilize their own parents in order to feel needed and have someone to sustain. Conversely parents may cling to an adolescent and delay that departure if facing the loss of their own dying parents. Another clinical issue of leaving home arises when families feel guilty if an elderly parent wants to live independent of them, seeks to make arrangements without their help, or perhaps lives with another elder. Societal norms, which urge adult children to assist aging relatives, often become translated into "make them dependent" and correspond with the limiting stereotype of the elder as a careneeder.

Problems of intergenerational boundaries and alliances are common within dysfunctional family systems, including those systems with elderly members. Adolescents are more likely to act out if grandparents who are present counteract parental orders. Intrusive grandparents may effect a breakdown of boundaries within the nuclear family. Members of the buffer generation may find themselves caught in the middle, feel helpless, and then function less effectively in any crises involving the elderly. Intergenerational conflict also may arise if the members of the older generation need to view their relations with their adult children as stable and dependable, while members of the middle generation experience these relationships as burdensome and problematic.

A clinical example of the latter point is the grandfather who kept producing problems for his adult children to solve, previously described in this chapter in the section on reframing. Another version of this situation is that in which an elder attempts to co-opt the responsibility for the adult children's problems, again both as an attempt to bolster a strong but shaken need for autonomy and independence and in an effort to free up the children's time and energy for the elder's own concerns.

Families should be observed for tendencies to magnify or to minimize the problems of the elderly (Duffy et al., 1982). Societal myths and stereotypes that predict inevitable decline in the elderly, coupled with a fear of the increasing dependency of the elder, can precipitate responses of overreaction and then incapacitation. Conversely, families may minimize the importance of observed changes in the elder. This then creates a family style of avoidance and delayed action for problem resolution, with attitudes that deny the reality of the elder's changes and assume instead a return to former functioning:

> Families' own myths of elderly parents always being strong and invulnerable and self-sufficient run parallel to family expectations that the intensity of family life will decrease as the children grow and leave home. In reality the problems associated with the process of aging oppose that assumption. (Duffy et al., 1982)

Traditional Family Therapy

A prevailing point of view expressed by many writers and clinicians in the field of family therapy focuses upon facilitating the differentiation of the young or middle-aged adult from the older generations; that is, from the prescriptions, prohibitions, projections, and conflicts transmitted from the past. This seems to assume that change is unidirectional, moving from the young to the old. But if we believe that old age is a developmental stage, this assumption becomes invalid. Older people can continue to grow and to differentiate themselves, and can help younger members do the same. The following case example illustrates this point:

> A 36-year-old man returned home to live with his 70-year-old parents after his mother had undergone cancer surgery and his father had a mild heart attack. The son developed a number of serious emotional difficulties, and his parents assumed a caretaking role for him. This effectively muted the family's concern about the aging parents' illnesses and possible death. The entire family proceeded to become stuck in a way that deterred everyone, including the parents, from moving on with their lives.
>
> In this case, the elders were encouraged to understand that their own life goals and development were hampered by the unresolved issues with their adult children. As they were helped to work on their long-standing marital issues and reach agreement and comfort about their own goals, they also began to arrive at new relationships with their sons. The family together could now face its concerns and fears about the future. The sons were freed to resume their own lives while remaining available to their parents in a new and supportive way.

In the case cited above, change began with the older generation and moved toward the younger members. It is crucial to remember that older members of families can and should be drawn in as full participants in efforts to help alleviate family difficulties. Developmental tasks, growth, and change are interactional in their effect upon the family system and can best be resolved through a mutual understanding involving all of the generations. The family systems stance is that it is the family who is the client, not the elder or some other member, and all members make important contributions.

WHOSE PROBLEM IS IT?

Herr and Weakland (1979) stressed that those attempting to solve the problems associated with aging should view them in relation to the elder's social support system. The primary social support for most people, including elders, is the family or extended kin network.

The field of family therapy is continually being developed and refined. It is now time to expand the earlier view to a further understanding that when an elder has a clinical problem, it may represent a problem in the person's social support system. The corollary also holds true, that when the presenting problem is attributed to an individual or family, that problem could be related to issues of the aging of an older family member. Thus at referral an essential question to be posed is: Whose problem is it?

First, let us begin with the situation where the presenting complaint is clearly defined by the referral source, and likely by the potential client as well, as being some problematic aspect of an elderly person. The human service provider needs to wonder immediately what other levels of dysfunction might also be present in the older adult's life, especially if the complaint is of either new or increased unacceptable behavior. As already indicated, individual elders may exhibit problems when their families are dysfunctional in aspects such as boundaries, hierarchy, roles and rules, and communication. Thus an individual assessment must also include a family or support system assessment. If the elder cannot provide full information, family members, a close friend, doctor, pastor, or neighbor may be valuable supplemental sources within the constraints of confidentiality. Because some older adults manifest confusion or impaired memory, these other informants can add details to the elder's situation and may also counterbalance any tendency of an emotionally impaired elder to misrepresent an earlier situation as though it is a current one. The attitudes mentioned in the earlier section on resistance by elders, and the statements that express these attitudes, must not deter the human service provider from obtaining the needed family data and involvement. Conversely, elders frequently enjoy reminiscing and giving their history; the task of the human service provider in these instances is to watch for gaps in the data and to guide the older adult to give as complete a picture as possible.

The other dimension of "Whose problem is it?" encompasses the all too frequent situation in which the needs of the elderly are unaddressed because the human service provider meeting with a younger family member attends solely to that individual's intrapersonal issues. By now our message must be clear that whenever *any client* requests treatment, a family assessment should be done. That assessment should include attention not only to younger family members but also to older ones. One needs to know if an elder member is interacting with family expectations based on myths of aging that alienate the elder and are stressful for the younger family members.

SUMMARY

Now the stage is set. Presenting problems are examined in systemic, not linear terms. Problems are reframed in a way that renders them solvable. The importance of joining with the family and its members receives full attention. The practitioner is alert to ageism and other obstacles to involving the elderly in treatment, including how their issues may be clouded by concerns of other family members. And the clinician is prepared to decide who should be included in treatment sessions.

These factors constitute the foundation of therapy. The course of treatment flows from how the problem is examined. Before proceeding to the next chapters for an exploration of assessment and subsequent interventions, we suggest that the human service provider use the following exercises to practice setting the stage for family-centered therapy with the elderly.

EXERCISES

1. Think of several families you know whose members have problems. (Choose families with at least one older adult member.) For each family, describe their problem(s) first in a linear framework of cause and effect. Then assess the same problem(s) again, this time in terms of the family as a system. (Be sure to include the function of the problem in maintaining family stability. What would the family have to address or resolve if the presenting problem(s) did not exist?)

2. Now that you are aware of the functions of the problems in the families you identified for Exercise 1, develop a workable goal that would address the needs of the various members of one of the families. (This will involve some reframing of the problem.)

3. What would be some important ways to join with or engage the family members, especially the older adults?

4. Using the following list, compose questions that should be asked in relation to each item when an older person with a problem is being assessed. Then go through the list again and write the questions to be asked for each item, this time when the client with the problem is another family member. Include your underlying hypotheses or concerns that you are attempting to validate.

- Intrafamilial resources
- Societal resources
- Family roles
- Precipitants of contact with the human service providers

5. In compiling questions in the above exercise, you will have sometimes written the same question to ask both the older adult and the other family member. What conclusions do you make about assessing the family when (a) the presenting problem is identified as that of an elder member, and (b) the problem is attributed to another family member?

6. How may the elderly be underserved if family issues or implications are ignored?

Chapter 3

FAMILY ASSESSMENT

INTRODUCTION

The purpose of this chapter is to focus on the content and the process of assessing older adults, their families, and their problems. The framework for assessment that we describe is consistent with the eco-systemic perspective presented earlier in Chapter 1. Both interior and exterior aspects of the family are addressed in relation to the generation and the resolution of the problem.

Constructivism, a recent entry into the field of family therapy, is examined for its relevance to the practitioner's stance and role in assessment. We then clarify some assumptions on which the framework for assessment and its process rest. Specific aspects of family life and experience, as well as the helping process itself, are given special attention. We then draw from traditional family therapies some techniques of structure, communication, and systems that we apply to the assessment of older clients and their families. An integral part of this chapter is the presentation of tools and techniques of assessment, with illustrations. For those not familiar with the necessary components of a family assessment, an outline appears at the end of the text as Appendix A.

Our material lays a foundation not only for assessment, but also for the beginnings of change. The assessment process is the first step of change; it shares with the process of treatment the same base. Treatment per se is delineated in detail in Chapter 4.

AN ECO-SYSTEMIC, CONSTRUCTIVIST FRAMEWORK

Our framework for assessment as well as for intervention and change rests on an eco-systemic perspective. As we detailed earlier in Chapter 1, a wide contextual lens is employed in the process of "knowing" the problems and the resources of older clients. Both problems and solutions are to be understood as components of the complex network of relationships involving the individual, the family system, and larger systems. In recent years, the field of family therapy has been flooded with ideas from constructivist theories. Our approach to assessment as well as to intervention is influenced by several of these ideas. (See Chapter 4 for interventions leading to change.) These concepts are consistent with an eco-systemic perspective and clinical work with older adults and their families.

Constructivism is a culturewide phenomenon that challenges our notions of reality and objectivity. Constructivists hold that reality is not discovered but is invented. An individual's view of reality is constrained by the perceptual frame or perspective that the person brings to the situation. In other words, we comprehend what we are able to comprehend, which is always an edited version of the "truth." The theories and experiences of the therapist determine how the family and its problems are perceived and addressed. For example, a structural family therapist will assess the family in terms of structural problems; interventions will take the form of restructuring.

From a constructivist point of view, the therapist is recognized as one of the players along with family members and other participants who co-create a therapeutic system. One of the practitioner's roles in assessment is to elicit the multiple realities about a problem and its resolution. A major question for assessment becomes, How does everyone make sense of the problem and the family at this point in time? Change may begin as the participants, including the clinician, teach each other the meaning they give the problem, what sense they make of their lives in relation to the problem, and their ideas about solutions to the problem. Change proceeds as the therapeutic system generates new realities.

A most useful result of the constructivist influence is the shift toward a collaborative stance between the practitioner and the client. As therapists have recognized that they are inescapably participants rather than observers in the therapeutic process, they have assumed a more egalitarian and less expert position with clients. This is a stance that is empowering of older clients because it validates them as the authority on their own lives, needs, and problems. It also invites the participation of family members and respects their "truths." The collaborative approach does not negate the clinician's knowledge and theories; rather, it makes that expertise more available for adding options to be considered. The difference is that the therapist's voice becomes one among many. The practitioner acts *with* rather than *on* the family.

Our use of constructivist theory is tempered by our belief that a sense of reality is contextual. Individuals may create their own realities but only within the constraints of the family and larger systems with which they coexist. Individuals, families, and larger systems are continually interacting. They influence each other in terms of values, premises, perceptions, and even opportunities. Power differences lend more credence and acceptability to some truths than to others. For instance, voices of the elderly, women, and nonwhites are not as likely to be heard as are those of young white males.

A part of assessment, therefore, focuses on understanding what White and Epston (1990, p. 9) term the "lived experience" of older adults. We address how elders have developed their experience as older men and women from different ethnic and racial groups. Our focus is in part on how the meanings that older adults make of this experience are related to their feelings about themselves, the problems that they face, and their attempts to change their lives in desired ways.

Assessment in the Continuum of Change

Assessment is the beginning of the change process. It is not the diagnosis of biological and emotional ills of the older client, even though we do not deny their importance. Rather the focus is on the evolving understanding of the interplay between the problem and the context in which it was generated and will be alleviated. For example, is the depression of the older person triggered by loss, either physical or emotional? How is the older adult's life changed by the depression? How are relationships different? Who knows of the depression? Who is affected by it and how? These questions plumb the effect of the depression on the lives of the older person, the family members, and others of significance. The inquiries also surface resources and supports that facilitate change.

Assessment, as the process of gathering needed information and of knowing, cannot be separated from the evolving patterns of therapy and of change. Assessment is, of course, an integral part of the whole. In our view the practitioner's approach to assessment, to "knowing" the family and the problem, sets the tone for everything else that is to occur. As we suggest above, the tone can be empowering if an atmosphere of mutual respect and partnership is promoted between clients and therapist. Whether this happens depends, to a great extent, on what the therapist brings to the situation by way of a belief system about families and about how to conduct therapy. The practitioner wedded to an expert stance owns the assessment process and is in charge of deciding which information is most relevant. The client's story and sense of reality may be ignored and/or discounted.

The collaborative approach that we recommend requires the laying aside of theoretical lenses, if only temporarily, in the interest of learning how the clients make sense of the world and what has happened to them. As Minuchin (1991) has said, "What keeps the honest therapist humble is not the realization that the truth is necessarily unknowable, but that it is always partial" (p. 50). The special knowledge that the practitioner brings and that clients expect becomes one partial truth among the many put forward by all who participate in the assessment process. Multiple perspectives voiced during the process can help define a workable problem and realistic solutions.

Assumptions

The assumptions upon which we base our approach to assessment of older adults and their families can be summarized as follows:

- A central focus for assessment is the understanding and validation of family strengths.
- Families generate their own norms for intergenerational relationships and living arrangements, based on current circumstance, family history, and ethnicity. There are no "right" norms for all families.
- Assessment is a collaborative and empowering process.
- Problems of older adults can be fully understood and resolved only in the context of the family and larger systems.
- The assessment process is often a trigger for needed change.

The remainder of this chapter is devoted to a presentation of what to assess in families and the tools and techniques for doing so. These are in keeping with the assumptions identified above.

A FRAMEWORK FOR FOCUS AND ASSESSMENT

Family assessment is a complex task. It is more than a search that results in the uncovering of a single cause or a single solution for a problem. Rather, it requires the understanding of the inner workings of a system that is multifaceted and constantly evolving. It often means learning of the family's perception of its development and functioning with respect to the larger society in which it is embedded. This is the backdrop against which the generation of the presenting problem and the potentials for solution come into focus during assessment.

Family therapists are aware of how easy it is to become overwhelmed with the mass of information that can be produced in conversations with families. This may be especially true with families of older adults who are often seen at times of crisis, when emotions run high. The concept of the "presenting edge" is a useful guide for focus and clarity during these times.

Lynn Hoffman (1983) has described the presenting edge as "that point of most tension between therapist and client" (p. 50). She has developed a tool, called the Time Cable, which organizes focal points of assessment into time and space "edges." The temporal edges pertain to the "differences in family patterns over time and how they relate to the presence of a symptom" (p. 50). Spatial edges refer to those persons and organizations significant to the generation and alleviation of the problem. The Time Cable is easily adapted as an aid in the assessment of the problems of older adults in the context of family and community life. Figure 3.1 is a diagram of this tool adapted for use with families of older adults.

We do not present this tool as one that requires rigid adherence on the part of the practitioner. It is meant to be a sensitizing agent as the therapist listens to the family tell its story of the problem and of the family experience in relation to the problem. The tool can serve as a guideline for identifying and bringing focus to the various presenting edges whenever the assessment process seems to be "stuck."

In this chapter we have organized the specific content areas of assessment using the Time Cable as a framework. We suggest that the practitioner keep the diagram in mind as a resource for ensuring the flow of information and understanding.

Space Edges   Time Edges

Family Helping: Future:
1. Meaning of needing help   1. What fears are there if problem
   Outside & family   not resolved?
2. Feared consequences   2. How will future be changed by
   Who will know?   involvement in this situation?
   What will be required?   3. What would you like your life to
   Will I lose control?   be like in 2-5 years?
3. Consequences of family involvement   4. How would you like family
   Increased responsibility   relationships to change in 5
   Stir up trouble   years?
   "Bring us too close"   5. What is your biggest worry?
   "Drive us apart"
                                                                               Present:
Family Dynamics: 1. What is problem?
1. Relationship edge   Different descriptions
2. Boundary edges   2. What are consequences of
   Inner/outer   problem?
3. Communication edge   What has changed?
4. Inter-generational edge   3. Who is involved?
5. Sibling edge   4. What is needed?
                                                                                  Different perspectives?
Referring Context:
1. Who referred?   Past:
2. Relationship to client   1. How does family history affect
3. Expectations   problem-solving?
                                                                               2. What models of care-giving in
Socio-Cultural Context: family of origin?
1. Societal edge   3. What are models of aging?
2. Meaning of aging   4. What values & premises are
3. Ethnicity & meaning   helpful/harmful now?
4. Gender meanings   5. What relationship resources are
                                                                                  there?

Labels within the figure: Socio-Cultural Context, Referring Context, Therapist/Agency, Family Dynamics

Figure 3.1. Edges of Assessment

SOURCE: Reprinted from *Diagnosis and Assessment in Family Therapy,* p. 50, with permission of
Aspen Publishers, Inc., @ 1983.

A STARTING POINT—THE MEANING OF HELP

The process of understanding, of knowing, the elderly person and the
family begins with a consideration of the meaning of seeking help. What
does it mean to be in the position of needing help from outside the
family resources? This is a question often overlooked in assessment
because of an eagerness to move quickly to problem solving and/or a
fascination with family and individual dynamics. The practitioner addressing the "meaning edge" will begin to identify family premises
about helping and caretaking, fears about family involvement, and areas
of conflict and difference within the family unit.

There are two prominent "edges" to be addressed early in the assessment. One involves whatever is activated within the family about the
need for outside help. The other examines what is activated between the

family and the practitioner in terms of the possibility for building a working partnership. Whether the practitioner is sensitive to such issues may determine the quality of the relationship between family and therapist. In a sense, assessment starts with the therapist asking, What does it mean for this family to be seeing me? What is going on in this family with respect to the referral for help? For its part, the family is probably coming with unspoken questions such as: Does this therapist understand how hard it is for us to come here? and What is this therapist up to?

Family Premises About Helping

Most families have operating premises about seeking help within the family and/or outside the family. These are not necessarily conscious ideas but can be ascertained by listening to the language and dialogue of the family. For example, when asked how they typically handle concerns about the elderly parents in the family, family members may jokingly reply, "We just call Fran, our older sister." This is a clear indication that Fran has been designated to be a caretaker and is a force to be reckoned with in the family. She maintains the duties and also the power that often accompanies the caretaker role. This may be a signal that the "whens" and "hows" of helping are to be cleared through Fran. Helpers from outside the family would do well to take this system into account.

Family members often share a belief system that indicates when it is appropriate to ask for help, to whom it is appropriate to turn for help, and what constitutes help. As we pointed out in Chapter 2, beliefs about helping can often prove to be an obstacle to obtaining needed help. Because such beliefs are crucial in the assessment process, we now revisit this issue in some detail.

Beliefs about helping have largely been shaped by the intergenerational family system, by ethnic heritage, and by the family's own life experiences regarding help. McGoldrick, Pearce, and Giordano (1982) point out, for example, that many middle-class white Americans have an individual orientation that stresses autonomy and an approach of "standing on your own two feet" (p. 40). Needing help is often considered a weakness and a failure. Many older adults of this tradition resist admitting the need for help, especially if the problems are emotional or interpersonal. Seeking or accepting help is not congruent with their perception of a life story of independence and self-reliance. Talking about such problems not only violates their sense of privacy and their norms of keeping family business within the family, but it also raises the levels of guilt and fear. Practitioners who seek to involve family members in the helping process may hear the older adult say, "I don't want to burden my children. They have their own lives to worry about. They depend on us for help. I vowed never to drag the children down with my worries." Fears of losing contact with their grown children are to be heard in comments such as, "I see little of my kids now. If they have to take on my troubles, I'll never see them."

An individual orientation contrasts with the value of interdependence and connectedness held by other groups. The family culture of these latter groups usually has well-developed, mutual helping systems that include extended family members, friends, and others. Boyd-Franklin (1989, p. 82), for example, speaks of the kinship network and the "church family," which can be important helpers in African-American families. Assessment should include identification of these helpers for the specific older adult in need of assistance. It is often wise to include them as part of the therapeutic partnership because they can be resources and catalysts for change.

For a further discussion of clinical aspects of ethnic differences, the reader is referred to Chapter 4.

Outmoded Family Premises

Another question of assessment is: To what degree are family premises helpful in the current life stage and circumstances of the family? Premises about depending solely on oneself and even on one's family may be outmoded when an elderly person is experiencing serious physical and emotional difficulties. An example of such a situation is that of an 80-year-old woman who exhausted herself with caretaking responsibilities for her 90-year-old husband rather than letting their daughter know of her father's dementia. This older couple lived close to the daughter but had clung rigidly to an old family premise not to "get into each other's hair" (Montalvo & Thompson, 1988, p. 32). It became clear that the family needed to develop appropriate ways to update this premise about each other and about resources outside family boundaries.

Even though families may have a well-developed mutual aid system within the family and its social network, they are not exempt from stress about seeking help. They too may need to examine the adequacy of their natural helping system. Sometimes the network breaks down. Younger people may, in the process of acculturation or for other reasons, no longer adhere to the family values of mutual help. Sometimes the very strength of the mutual aid system cuts off necessary help from the outside, perhaps from fear of loss of control or from lack of knowledge about the options. There are also situations in which the stress of the older person is related to continuing to accept responsibilities in the caretaking network long after the capacity to do so has diminished. One 72-year-old grandmother devoted most of her resources to the care of her daughter's children. She began to experience increasing physical symptoms, but did not share her concerns with her family. The daughter, a single mother, was unaware of the toll exacted from her mother. She depended on her mother's help and had come to take it for granted. In this case, the grandmother was in need of help, but the reciprocity upon which mutual aid rests had deteriorated.

Family Culture

The meaning of accepting help is complex, requiring sensitivity to the family culture. The practitioner must be prepared to listen to the voice of the family in this respect. Some questions that may be helpful are the following:

- What usually happens in your family when someone needs help?
- What is your past experience with outside helpers?
- What has helped in the past? What has not helped?
- Did your parents need help in their old age? What did you do (asked of the older adult)?
- Who in the family agrees that outside help is required now?
- What does needing help outside the family mean to you about yourself?
- Will seeking help outside the family change your relationship with anyone significant to you? How?
- Who in the extended family and your network knows of your contact with this agency?

Factors of Gender

A factor to be considered in understanding the meaning of help is that of gender. Men more than women may have trouble seeking help because most males have been socialized to value autonomy and independence. Seeking help is often an anathema to men and contradicts their view of masculinity. Being dependent does not fit their life story even though most have spent much of their lives depending on women. Dependency needs in many of these men have largely gone unacknowledged and can be a threatening proposition (Meth & Pasick, 1990). Perhaps this is a reason that clinicians often find that problems with elderly couples are focused on the older woman. Clinicians should be aware that this focus can mask difficulties with the male. A "symptomatic" wife may inadvertently be providing a recently retired man with a new project or second career.

Personal Meanings of Family Participation

Another assessment edge, or focus, with respect to the significance of help is related to the real or perceived consequences of family involvement. These are personal perceptions at the individual level as opposed to those at the family and cultural levels. When practitioners are experiencing difficulties in convening family members to discuss problems with an older parent or relative, it is wise to address this edge of meaning.

What does it mean to younger family members to be invited to address the difficulties of parents, grandparents, aunts and uncles? Let us suppose, for example, that young or middle-aged adults have been estranged or even totally cut off from their older relatives. Often such situations result from unresolved emotional issues within the family. As we mentioned in Chapter 2 when discussing obstacles to treatment, the younger "adult children" are likely to be reluctant to be drawn back into a situation of emotional involvement with the older parents. To be asked to do so brings up fears of being overwhelmed or manipulated or made to feel guilty—the same issues that distanced them from their parents and/or their siblings in the first place. When asked to meet with his elderly father, one man said, "I'll contribute money but don't ask for more. We didn't get along when I was young and it's too late now. He didn't approve of me then. Let sleeping dogs lie. It's too painful for us all." Another said, "Talking will just drive us further apart. Let's leave it alone." In these cases, the meaning of becoming involved in the helping process is pain.

A focus on what it means for younger adults to become involved in helping older family members can uncover many premises about what is acceptable to talk about within the family. Younger people may be reluctant to become involved because of a sense of violating family norms. There may be an assumption that one does not pry into others' business or that one does not ask questions about painful topics. Participating in family discussions raises the fearful specter of penetrating forbidden areas and violating rules of communication. (Communication processes will be discussed more fully later in this chapter.)

Highlighting the meaning of help may reveal that the powerful positions of one or more family members are threatened by outside helpers. A caretaker may need relief but also may hesitate to turn control over to anyone else. Families who pride themselves on their closeness may perceive outsiders as being meddlers intent upon and powerful enough to separate them, perhaps by hospitalizing the older person or by placing the elder in a nursing home. This concern is especially prevalent in families whose accepted practice dictates that older people are cared for by the family.

One consequence to participation that sometimes is overlooked in assessment is the consequence for a primary caretaker. Caretakers are usually adult daughters. Both they and the family may take for granted the "naturalness" of this role for women. Yet most women today are employed outside the home. Therefore it has become necessary to consider the effects of caring for older parents on the adult daughter's life and on the lives of her spouse and children. Questions that will indicate whether she is overloaded and overwhelmed are in order. A family discussion can be helpful in assessing how her spouse/partner and her children are experiencing the increased demands on her time. A most important topic is what supports she needs and what are available to her.

Some questions to trigger discussion of the individual meaning of involvement with older persons and their problems are the following:

- What is your biggest worry about meeting with other family members?
- What is your biggest concern about talking with people outside the family about this matter?
- How do you think becoming involved in these discussions will affect your life?
- What is your biggest worry about not becoming involved?
- How is your caretaking role affecting your life and the lives of those closest to you?

Personal Fears and Family Dilemmas

Another issue at the meaning level of helping may be a belief that if we talk about it, it will come true, or, at the very least, it will get worse if we talk about it. Discussions of some of the difficulties facing elderly people can be extremely frightening when the family holds such a premise. For example, one woman became concerned about some symptoms of difficulty in breathing and some chest pain that her 78-year-old father was experiencing. She felt compelled to urge her parents to seek an evaluation. Her mother initially resisted the evaluation, but later became convinced of the need to make arrangements for it. The result was a diagnosis of heart disease. The mother became angry with her daughter and accused her of making them face something for which they were unprepared. In her words, "I knew what it was but you forced us to have a diagnosis. We were doing fine. Now what will we do?"

The several dilemmas represented in this vignette make it important for the practitioner to spend time with the family members at this juncture. Assessment in this case revealed that the parents had managed many problems such as alcoholism and marital conflict through a system of denial. From their point of view, the family was protected from dire consequences, including divorce, by ignoring problems. Acknowledging problems and involving outside helpers almost always meant facing decisions about staying together or disrupting the family. For this older couple, "looking the other way" suited their purpose. Their experience had taught them that situations do not necessarily improve by talking about them. The adult daughter, a social worker, had learned to challenge the family premises in her own life because they had proved to be dysfunctional for her. She turned to therapists and a process of talking things through in her life and with her spouse and children. Thus she had earned in her family of origin the reputation of being someone who always stirs up trouble by talking. For her parents, the recent event was further proof of their view.

The practitioner who offered help to this family was faced with the dilemma of two opposing questions: How could help be given? and Who is right? This was a family in which both aspects of the question held some truth. Assessment revealed the partial truths and their functionality for each family member. Assessment in this instance brought to light multiple perspectives and options for change. As often happens in this kind of assessment, the practitioner took the opportunity to add another perspective. She pointed out that there is no guarantee that talking about problems solves them. She noted that talking often seems to make a problem worse when people are revealing pain for the first time. She added, too, that a certain amount of denial of problems or looking the other way may even be functional, especially in older adults who face multiple fears and stresses. Then, drawing upon her experience with others in similar situations, she observed that a point is reached beyond which looking the other way may become harmful. Older people can become cut off from supports that may enhance their quality of life. By using the language of the family, the therapist thus hoped to affirm the older couple while opening up the possibility of seeing another view of their traditional way of facing problems and change.

This case example highlights another reason that helping triggers emotionally intense responses. Helping another sometimes requires shifting personal boundaries. Although we address the assessment of family boundaries later in this chapter, the relevance of boundaries for issues of helping warrants some mention here. The daughter thought that she had a legitimate need to know, which the parents experienced as a violation of their private boundary. For the parents, part of the meaning of accepting help from inside or outside the family pertained to making their business public. There is no question that the balance between what is public and what is private will change within the family, and between the family and the external world, when outside helpers enter the picture. Part of assessment in this case focused on facilitating the family's recognition of their premises regarding public versus private boundaries. Assessment identified shifts that would be necessary and acceptable for receiving adequate help.

Following are some guidelines that may prove helpful in assessing the personal meanings of help described above:

- Openly address and acknowledge the difficulties and the risks involved. Talking and doing can be painful. Change is frightening but will happen anyway.
- Help the family sort through options (what if they do X, what if they don't do X), so that alternatives can emerge.
- When faced with decisions such as the one in the vignette above, use specific questions such as:
    What worries you about doing it?
    What worries you about not doing it?
    How will it be better or worse for each family member either way?
    Which situation is more tolerable for you?

Who could help you with this decision?

What will help you with this decision? Talking, ruminating, praying?

- When possible, urge the family members to take time to think things through and to consult others.

The intent of these guidelines is to empower the family members by activating their own problem-solving mechanisms. This step should reveal to them where there are gaps. Note that the practitioner is not making interpretations. The focus is on helping the family members realize their own reality and its meaning. Part of the assessment process involves facilitating family discussion with the ensuing recognition of the members' own needs and resources.

PROBLEM IDENTIFICATION

Earlier, in Chapter 2, we spoke of the importance of defining and reframing the presenting problem in a workable way as a critical step in setting the stage for change. A glance at the Time Cable diagram in Figure 3.1 reveals that a primary edge to be addressed early in the assessment is the present experience of the family, especially relative to members' problems. Our focus at this point is the meaning of the problem within the family and its impact on the family as an organization. The clinician should understand the role of the family in defining an event or situation as a problem. How the family views itself in relation to the problem and to its solution is equally important. A discussion of the problem should yield information regarding the level of agreement among family members about the problem, how the family has changed as a result of the problem, who is doing what about it, and who feels most affected by it. In addition, a picture of the alliances and conflictual relationships may begin to emerge. The ideas and the resources within the family for alleviating the stressful situation become apparent.

Hoffman (1985) stated that a problem does not reside in family organization or inside an individual, but is located instead in an "ecology of ideas." This notion is consistent with the view that we advanced earlier in this chapter about the assumptions and stance of the practitioner. A problem is, in a sense, what those who have an interest in it agree that it is. For example, stress-producing conversation about an event lends shape to that event as a problem. An event takes on meaning and definition as a problem from the way it stresses the resources and the life experience of all of those affected by it. We do not deny that certain physical and emotional symptoms and diagnoses exist. Our focus, however, is on the process of an event becoming problematic for the specific individual and the family.

There are many aspects to problem definition. A family's many definitions depend on how each member experiences the problematic event. This leads the assessor to ask a set of questions of everyone who is involved:

- What is the problem at this point?
- How is this a problem for you?
- How has this family become different since the event?
- How has your life become different since this event occurred?
- Who in the family agrees that this is a problem?
- What change would you like to see?
- What do you believe would be most helpful in bringing about the change(s)?

Questions such as these clarify the meaning of the problem in terms of the impact it has had on people's lives. Out of the inquiry comes the story that is building in the family about the problem and about the person who has been identified as having it. A role of the practitioner is to surface the multiple descriptions and the level of agreement and disagreement about them. From the many voices, a workable definition is constructed. To achieve this, the practitioner must cultivate a respectful curiosity (Cecchin, 1987, p. 407) with which to devise creative questions.

The practitioner's voice is not silent; instead it furthers the conversation and the assessment by offering alternative descriptions. Not unlike the intervention of positive connotation presented later in Chapter 4 on treatment, a perspective could be offered that normalizes the problem as stress associated with a life transition. The clinician then might go on to suggest some ideas about what seems to maintain or exacerbate the problem. The family could be helped to examine behavioral sequences related to the problem. The therapist could help the family construct alternative explanations about the problem, about the older person identified with the problem, and/or about the family. The therapist's voice is one that invites the older client and the family to consider these ideas as possibilities and not as the "truth." This kind of approach empowers the family and facilitates their involvement not only in the assessment process but also in the ongoing efforts toward change.

In the process of the discussion described above, the practitioner begins to learn, too, of the family organization. It will, for example, become relatively clear who holds power in this family. The therapist need only note who possesses the power to define problems and solutions. Whose voice is heard and whose is silenced? What is the consequence in each instance? This conversation at the edge of problem identification may also begin to reveal roles such as that of the family caretaker. These roles will be addressed in some detail when we discuss family structure later in the chapter.

PAST HISTORY AND FUTURE POSSIBILITIES

Part of the effort to understand the problem may require conversational journeys into the past or into the future. These edges of time may be important for determining how and why the problem is defined in the way it is. The intergenerational history of a family is an active component in the current life of any family, whether or not it is acknowledged as such. For example, expectations and belief systems about health, illness, and difficulties in relation to aging can be rooted in past generations. Models of aging and of caregiving, passed from one generation to the next, often influence attitudes and relationships of younger and older generations of the family.

Genogram

We recommend the construction of a genogram, an intergenerational map of the family, as a routine part of assessment with older clients and their families. Most practitioners are familiar with this tool. For those who are not, we offer a brief description of the procedure and the process.

The genogram is an intergenerational map of three or more generations of a family. Each sibling set is plotted horizontally with a vertical line connecting it with the parental generation. A square is used to indicate a male, a circle for a female, and a triangle when the gender is unknown. The last situation may occur in the case of an abortion, a miscarriage, or an instance of the client being uncertain about the facts. The names and the dates of birth and death are placed within each symbol. Words that identify characteristics, traits, and significant data can be recorded directly below the symbol. A solid line connecting a square to a circle indicates a marriage, while a broken line signals an unmarried couple who live together. A double hatch mark across either line symbolizes divorce or separation. Deaths are indicated by drawing a line through the square, circle, or triangle. Significant family relationships are diagrammed by identifying cutoffs and triangles. For those who lack experience with the genogram, many references are available that offer detailed instructions (see Hartman & Laird, 1983; McGoldrick & Gerson, 1985). Appendix B provides a sample genogram, that of the Berry family, our case example in Chapter 1.

The therapist takes the lead in the construction of the genogram by eliciting the necessary information and by recording the information on a large sheet of paper. The size of the paper is important because the genogram is a document that is usually developed throughout the course of therapy. A central role for the practitioner in the mapping process is to encourage family members to add to the discussion, to ask questions of the older members, to tell family stories, and to share emerging feelings. An intergenerational picture of family values, patterns, myths, and premises will evolve. Older adults and their families often gain new perspectives about their problems when viewed against a backdrop that shows intergenerational patterns of aging, attitudes about aging and the elderly, and models of caregiving.

Construction of a genogram can be an empowering experience for the older person who is usually the authority on family history. It is a time for younger generations to become acquainted with the life stories of their forebears and to recognize their influence on the identity of today's family. Adult children and grandchildren may gain a different perspective about the older adult as his or her earlier life story and family roles emerge. Younger generations may glimpse strengths never before recognized in a parent, especially in one with whom relationships have been strained.

The structure afforded by constructing the genogram facilitates discussion. In this process, people often have the opportunity to ask specific questions for the first time. One woman revealed to her mother how sad and angry she had felt when her mother had accepted a job as a secretary when she, the daughter, was just 4 years old. She asked why her mother had done this because her father was financially successful. Her mother, surprised, explained that she had decided to work to ensure that her three daughters would have the college educations that she had missed. Needless to say this explanation cast the experience in a different and more positive light for the daughter and helped to heal a sore spot in the relationship.

Adult children can be helped to understand, if not excuse, actions of an older parent when they perceive that parent in the context of his or her early family experience. One man, for example, learned for the first time that his father, as a young child, had experienced physical abuse at the hands of his own father. The father explained how, as a result, he feared that his own anger might spill over into abuse. Consequently he tried to maintain tight control of his emotions. He felt that he could best protect his children by not getting too close to them even though he loved them. This revelation did not heal all the past grievances, but it did provide a building block for a stronger relationship between father and son.

The genogram can identify resources and connections in the extended family. The ecomap, to be discussed more fully later in this chapter, can also be helpful in mapping these connections. Whichever tool is used, siblings of the older adult are particularly noteworthy; the strength and influence of the sibling bond is just beginning to be recognized. Siblings of the older adult may prove to be valuable sources of information, but more importantly, they may provide emotional support and other resources for their relative. Many practitioners find that inviting siblings of the older person to the sessions can initiate change. It is never too late to work out unresolved emotional issues from the past. Many older adults are quite capable of bridging old family cutoffs, renewing emotional connections, and healing past wounds.

The genogram does not need to be confined to a study of the past. After constructing it, the practitioner can ask the older person and the family to identify important present connections within the extended family. It can be useful for the family to explore who knows of the current problems and to speculate about how these individuals can be involved in planning or in problem solving. A discussion by the elder family members regarding the amount of contact they have within their family is usually significant. The older adult may tell others what kind of connectedness he or she would like in the future and with whom. Other questions to pose include: What kind of support does the older adult expect to need from extended family members in the future? How confident is the elder that such support will be available? What needs to be done to ensure the desired degree of contact and support?

Tapping the Future

Focus on the future in assessment helps the elder and the family members reveal to themselves and to others some of the worries and fears that influence their relationships. People often behave in the present on the basis of their unspoken projections of what they fear or hope the future may be. When the practitioner suspects this to be the case, questions such as What is your biggest worry about the future? and What are your fears if things go on as they are? can trigger an appropriate conversation. The therapist can also ask the family members to imagine themselves in two years, and to describe where they are and where they would like to be in relationship to each other. How would they like things to be the same, and how would they like things to be different? These discussions sometimes help develop alternative views and options for change.

Other questions that may be asked about the future are:

- If the current problem does not change, what do you predict will happen in this family?
- How do you think you will have to change in order to resolve the problem in the way you desire?
- Do you think you will be spending more or less time with your parent (your son/daughter) in the future? Why?
- What strengths are there in this family that you would never want to change?

FAMILY DYNAMICS

Until now, we have discussed understanding the family in terms of its view of the problem and its willingness to engage in the helping process along with the older member of the family. At some point, of course, the focus will shift to understanding the family itself as an operating unit. It is useful to understand the elderly family member's resources and limitations. What are the dynamics, the patterns that reveal the presenting problem? What can be done about them? The family is a major contextual factor in understanding the problems and in creating solutions. A family can be viewed as a small society with its own boundaries and its own governing rules. It has its own life story and its own set of values. Each family has its unique way of relating to the outside world of larger systems, as we mentioned in our earlier discussion of accepting help. If an outsider is to understand such a unit, a way must be found to access what amounts to foreign territory. The therapist is, in many ways, a stranger in a strange land and must learn to speak the language.

Imber-Black (1986, p. 150) has identified the inner language of the family as a resource. By inner language, we mean features such as words with special meanings, myths, metaphors, rituals, special foods, and family jokes. These factors identify the family members to themselves and to others. The language can be the key to a fuller understanding of the presenting problem and of possible solutions. We have already discussed earlier the use of language in joining with a family. Language is also a the key to the system of meaning within the family. "The therapist's intervention that is grounded in the family's inner language may, in fact, enhance the family's repertoire in this domain" (Imber-Black, 1986, p. 150). It is empowering when the therapist can use the inner language in appropriate ways and can help the family design change within its own framework for meaning.

The therapist must be able to put aside the inner language from his or her own family in order to hear another's. The practitioner can begin to understand the inner language by listening for key words, eliciting stories, and noting themes identified by the genogram. Familiarity with inner language is central to understanding family structure and organization, communication, and the family's emotional processes. These features are discussed in the following sections. Of course, this relationship is mutual as these aspects of the family also represent the inner language of the family.

STRUCTURE AND BOUNDARIES

Froma Walsh (1980) claims that "the successful functioning of families in later life requires a flexibility in structure, roles, and responses to new developmental needs and challenges" (p. 213). As we pointed out in Chapter 1, a central concept in family practice with older adults and their families is that of boundary. In this section we elaborate on the usefulness of focusing on boundary issues as a way of assessing many of the difficulties facing such families. A primary concern is how family patterns of closeness and distancing may contribute to and/or maintain the problem of a family member. The therapist explores workable alliances, troublesome triangles, power distribution, and hierarchy.

The assessment should give the practitioner a sense of the flexibility of the family structure, that is, the family's ability to be responsive to needed changes over time. The practitioner should be alert to signs that current boundary arrangements are no longer working well and need renegotiation. Every life transition involves the family in renegotiation of its boundaries. However, this topic can be especially difficult for families of the elderly to discuss because it usually entails facing painful and emotional issues.

One question for assessment is the relationship style, which is characterized by internal family boundaries. Some families tend to be overly close or enmeshed, while others tend toward overly distant or disengaged styles (Minuchin, 1974). Some may be a mixture of the two, to the extent that they contain individual examples of each. Stress activates these otherwise "invisible" boundaries, especially when it brings the family into contact with larger systems. Neither the enmeshed nor the disengaged style is necessarily a problem. The difficulty, however, is that these styles may become even more exaggerated in times of stress. The tendency of enmeshed families to overreact presents the danger of overprotecting or even infantilizing older family members, perhaps out of fear of potential loss. In those cases, younger family members may interfere with whatever autonomy and independence remains for the older adult. The younger person "doing for" or "doing to" rather than "with" the elder may remove the older adult from planning for his or her own needs. Conversely when disengagement is the style, family members may tend to avoid or ignore problems and needs of the older person. In those instances the older person may resort to dramatic means such as suicide attempts or flare-ups of serious illness to gain needed attention. Asking the older adult how and from whom needed family support is obtained will elicit pertinent information at this edge.

We are not taking the position that the boundary arrangements described above are indications of family pathology. These structures may have worked well for the family and its individual members for many years. Significant cultural factors may be at work in these customary arrangements. Rather, the practitioner's role during the assessment is to help the family determine how its usual way of doing business is either maintaining the current predicament or is hindering arrival at an effective solution.

A measure of family strength is whether the family possesses enough flexibility to modify its boundaries as members' developmental needs change over time. The following case history illustrates our point. Sandra Brown, a woman in her 50s, sought help for handling her concerns about her 82-year-old mother. Her parents lived about 60 miles from her and they lived alone. On a recent visit to another daughter, the mother awakened in a disoriented state and became very frightened. She revealed some concerns about her health, which had been kept secret prior to this time. As the eldest of four siblings and the one through whom information was sifted in time of trouble, Sandra was immediately contacted by her sister. Sandra was distressed and called her parents' home. Her father answered and told Sandra that he could handle whatever needed to be done and forbade her to visit or to tell her mother of her concerns. He said, "Do not upset your mother. There is nothing wrong." Sandra had never challenged her father on anything. She followed her mother's dictum, "Don't get your father angry." It had been her role to keep her father happy and smiling. She recalled how her mother had sent her to make Dad laugh when he was upset. How could she now handle her grave concerns when it meant going against his wishes?

As children, Sandra and her siblings feared their father and felt closer to their mother. In their adult years, they maintained only a perfunctory involvement with their father, seldom talking of anything meaningful. The lack of involvement may have protected them earlier because they thereby avoided his anger, which they feared would estrange them even more. But now this disengagement was threatening to escalate and cut off the two generations from each other in dangerous ways. At this stage of family life, disengagement was not working well. The boundary arrangement was outmoded and in need of renegotiation.

In the process of renegotiation of boundaries, most families face issues of hierarchy—power, authority, and control. They also encounter issues of connectedness, caring, and differentiation. Each of these areas involves not only the organization of intergenerational family life but also the key emotional processes in the family. The interrelationship between connectedness and separateness contributes to some of the difficulty and pain experienced in identifying boundary problems and in affecting necessary change.

Power, Authority, and Control

Williamson (1982) stated that there is a stage in the family life cycle that involves the termination of the hierarchical boundary between the first and second generations within a three-generational life cycle. This stage represents the final step in the evolving relationship between parents and child. The issues often concern power, autnority, and control. The direction of renegotiation of the relationship is toward equality with a more person-to-person flavor. In Sandra's case mentioned above, power and control were clearly pivotal. The father was the unquestioned authority. The women of the family had accommodated him in his role. This situation had eventually led to the daughters' being unavailable to him, both by their physical absence and emotionally, as they grew older and became independent.

Families differ with respect to hierarchy. Consequently they differ in the amount of strain experienced at boundaries as parents age. What is desired and what is realistic in terms of renegotiation of boundary issues must take cultural differences into account. Some families, notably single-parent families, may have developed a workable democratic style. In those families, power and control may not present a problem as the family members grow older.

One task for assessment is to help evaluate the nature and the quality of boundaries. Some questions to guide the therapist are:

- Who is the most powerful person in this family?
- Has this balance of power changed recently?
- Who feels powerful and why?
- How are decisions made in the family? If there is a disagreement, who prevails?
- How are elders involved in decision making?
- If a plan for different living arrangements for the older adult had to be made, who would make that decision?

A problem of power and authority occurs in families whose members do not acknowledge the growing disability of their elder member. To do so would threaten their image of this individual as the strong and protective head of the family. Unfortunately the nature of power is such that it often has a constitutive effect. In other words, it shapes the lives and beliefs of those involved, making inequities of power seem natural and removing from perception the option of seeing the world differently. One young man found it impossible to resist going on drinking binges with his alcoholic father even though the health of both men was severely threatened. His father was a tyrant and commanded his sons to act like men by proving that they could be "hard drinkers" as he and his father had been. The younger man idolized his father and his achievements as an attorney. It never occurred to him to question his father's behavior; that would have been perceived as an untenable breach of boundary. The younger man stood by his father even in the face of opposition from others in the family. To recognize his father as being alcoholic and out of control threatened his vision of his father as strong and in charge. To accept that reality, of course, also would have meant evaluating his own behavior in a different light.

An inability to breach the boundary of power between authoritarian parents and their adult children can be harmful for the whole family. The example of the father and the son is a case in point. Other examples include situations in which older parents need medications monitored and their children either ignore the situation or are fearful about confronting the parent. Many adults are reluctant to step forward and become assertive with a parent who has been remote, unavailable, and/or frightening in the past. Also operative may be the inability to face how old age is transforming the parent from the strong person upon whom one could always depend to the one who now needs help.

Older adults often seek to reinforce the rigid boundary of power by increasing their demands. These demands may simply be the elders' way of reassuring themselves that they still have the power to ensure that their needs are met. However, adult children may then complain in private, about the demanding quality of a parent. This conflict will most likely produce further distance in relationships that are already strained. One question to address in assessment is whether the demanding behavior represents a change. Has there been an increase in the demands or are they being experienced differently by the children? The clinician may reframe the elder's dictates as being an attempt to adapt to and master the situation of aging in the familiar way of exercising control. This technique is an example of positive connotation, an intervention for treatment as well as for assessment that we delineate further in Chapter 4.

Roles

What our discussion of power suggests is the need for close attention to roles in the family. Who have occupied positions of power in the family? Who has been the one to respond and in what ways? Has there been a sense of justice and fairness in the family in the past? How is the older person experiencing loss of control and power in the family? Is power a major issue?

Old resentments toward the elder family member will flare if issues of power and control are unresolved. The assessment should uncover such concerns and identify the potential for effecting appropriate change if the current needs of the elder are to be met. Understanding stress as it relates to boundary issues may present an opportunity to reframe problems in terms of normative stress and to begin the work of renegotiation.

A related issue to be addressed in the assessment is that of roles for older adults in the family. Carter and McGoldrick (1980) speak of the key emotional process of the family in later life as "accepting the shifting of generational roles" (p. 17). As we already mentioned in Chapter 2, some changes involved in completing this process are "support for a more central role for the middle generation" and "making room in the system for the wisdom and experience of the elderly." This framework suggests that older adults need not lose power in the shift in generational roles. Instead the family task is one of empowering its elder members. Older adults can be valuable resources for all members of the family. For example, some families depend upon grandparents for assistance with child care. A discussion of current roles for the elderly, as well as roles expected for the future, is significant.

Connectedness and Caring

Perhaps one of the most important aspects of families of older adults is the quality of connectedness and caring. These strengths are particularly critical at this life stage and warrant careful assessment. Karpel (1986, pp. 179-189) has identified family loyalty, affection, and reciprocity as family resources and strengths. Contemporary society in the United States emphasizes the differentiation of the young from their parents and values independence and autonomy. The need and the longing for connectedness is generally given short shrift. The ability to maintain quality connectedness, however, is a strength of well-functioning families.

Leaving Home

Certainly one task that all families face as its members grow older is that of how to stay connected. In most families, the expectation is that the children will grow and establish themselves in lives and households separate from their parents. How, when, and in what ways differ from ethnic group to ethnic group. A difference in expectations and socialization also exists in terms of gender. Males, by and large, are socialized to place more emphasis on autonomy and independence, although culture is a mediating factor here, too. Females, on the other hand, are more likely to be socialized into nurturing, caretaker roles that are based on interdependence.

An important assessment issue relates to expectations about differentiation. When do people leave home and under what conditions? Have there been rifts in the family about leave-taking? For example, one older parent had never forgiven his son for rejecting the family business 20 years earlier in order to follow a military career. The father's pride and pain proved to be difficult obstacles to his son's efforts to assume some responsibility for his father's needs in older age.

Filial Responsibilities

The level and quality of intergenerational connectedness throughout the family's early life cycle may set the stage for this later period. As parents age, a central shift for the adult children involves filial responsibility. The family must address the issue of how the children will support and care for the maturing family members, should care become a necessity. Questions to be posed are:

- How do adult children view their filial responsibilities?
- How do older parents view those responsibilities?
- How do previous relationships between parents and children support the acceptance of filial responsibility?
- Is this a family in which healthy interdependence is valued?
- What resources are available to support filial responsibility?
- What prevents healthy interdependency—jobs, children, other?

The examination of connectedness in families leads us to address pressures associated with the care of older parents. These pressures will undoubtedly raise the family's emotional issues that have been covered over but not resolved. One reason for this process is that the care of parents highlights dependence, not independence. The necessity of caring for needy older parents focuses adult children on their own dependency needs. Are they forced to care for a parent who, in their perception, did not care for them as children?

Suspected problems in areas of caring and connectedness should be allowed to surface for further assessment. Unresolved issues of nurturing and caring may remain for the parents and their adult children. Sometimes the resentment is hidden; sometimes it has disrupted the relationship for some time. One 65-year-old woman reported that she had had no contact with her daughter for 4 years. She had been a single mother who raised two children with very little support. Her daughter had long felt neglected and forced to care for herself from an early age. She blamed her mother for the divorce. At age 18 the daughter left for college, which ended what little communication had occurred between the two of them. The mother desired contact and hoped to heal the rift but felt powerless to do anything about it. Assessment clarified the issues and she was able to write a simple note that said: "I have missed you a great deal and feel much sadness about our lack of contact. I hope that some kind of relationship is still possible between us." The daughter responded, and, although much time was required, they were able to resolve many past hurts and grievances. Their relationship was revitalized to the benefit of both.

Siblings as a Resource

As we noted earlier with respect to the older generation, siblings of the middle generation can be an important resource for each other. Meeting with siblings during the assessment period can underscore the possibilities for change. However, old, unresolved emotional issues can also emerge. Feelings of favoritism of one child over another often surface in discussions of who is to care for an older parent. Siblings may have markedly different perceptions of their parents and different experiences in the family. As one woman said to her sister, "I know we are full sisters and neither of us is adopted, so how come you have a different father?" Assessment can help determine the sibling issues that need attention so that obstacles to helping can be removed. It is not unusual for one sibling to be designated as the family caretaker and the primary caregiver for elderly parents in need.

Some of the questions to be touched upon in assessment with the siblings are:

- What help does the primary caretaker need from the others?
- Who is seen in what role in the family?
- Are current roles functional or do they need to be changing?

Retirement and Disruption of Rituals

The life style of today's older adults may lead to interpersonal difficulties and problems of connectedness between them and their adult children. Assessment may focus increasingly on problems of family disruption generated by retirement. Many older parents are retiring early and enjoying good health and independence for years. Their desire to travel or to relocate is causing some difficulties. In some families, grandparents have been significantly involved in the care of their grandchildren, perhaps when a single parent goes off to work. One single mother complained bitterly that her parents were abandoning her when they announced plans to spend several months of every year in Arizona. Other adult children mourn the loss of family holiday rituals, which are disrupted because of the absence of older parents. These are serious considerations in families, and future connectedness is at stake.

COMMUNICATION

Communication is at the heart of emotional processes in the family. It is often cited as an area of difficulty between older parents and their families. Assessment typically should yield information about the degree of openness permitted—regarding the family, patterns of interaction among family members, family styles, and family taboos. Assessment usually reveals the presence of any of the following difficulties:

- long-established patterns and rules of family communication that are dysfunctional at the current life stage
- secret resentments that remain unexpressed verbally but often erupt behaviorally
- fear of hurting each other by expressing needs and desires
- fear of loss, especially on the part of older adults, if they express themselves openly

A study conducted by Feinauer, Lund, and Miller (1987) regarding intergenerational relationships in multigenerational households highlights the inability to communicate as a major dissatisfaction between older people and their adult offspring. The study identified several significant areas in which lack of communication seemed especially troublesome. Elders thought that others did not perceive them clearly. They felt unsure of what younger members thought of them and were uncertain how family members felt about them as aging individuals. More important, they were reluctant to talk about their feelings. Adult children consulted in the study expressed fears regarding their parents' aging and potential loss of independence. The principal worry was how their parents' aging might impact their own lives. They, too, found themselves unable to express these fears openly. As a result they often appeared angry and withdrawn and found themselves communicating less with their parents. Unfortunately the inability to talk about painful feelings often leads to misperceptions on the part of both generations.

A hazard of miscommunication is that people then act upon their perceptions without questioning their unconfirmed assumptions. In some instances the fears of adult children are based upon misconceptions about aging that cannot be clarified when it is impossible to speak of them. They may, for example, assume that aging automatically means dependency and failing intellectual and physical abilities. Some may even attempt to take over their parents' lives without consultation about the needs and desires of the older person. This kind of behavior, though well-intended, can result in pain and damaged relationships.

Therapists often hear examples of how misconceptions and dysfunctional patterns of communication increase stress between the older and younger generations. For example, one woman noted that her mother, recently widowed, seemed to be neglecting her housework. Without talking to her mother, the daughter appeared one day and cleaned her mother's home. To the daughter's surprise, her mother did not seem grateful and even appeared angry about the situation. Later discussion about this incident revealed that the older woman felt hurt and confused by her daughter's behavior. She assumed her daughter realized how depressed she had become about the death of her husband, although she had not spoken of it. She also began to wonder whether her daughter was noticing some failings that she herself had not recognized. She began to fret about loss of independence even though she was in good health. The daughter, who had also been grieving in silence, talked of her assumption that her mother's behavior was another sign of aging.

Her father had started to decline at the same age. Fearing another loss, she decided to take action. Both mother and daughter explained that they had not talked to each other about the sadness over their mutual loss because, "in our family, we don't like to upset each other by talking of sad things."

The above situation illustrates a common difficulty in communication between the generations. Over the years, families develop patterns and rules about communicating with one another. These reflect intergenerational and cultural styles. They include acceptable standards of expressing anger, affection, needs, and wants. They include taboos, topics that are unacceptable in open discussion. The degree of openness between older and younger generations varies from family to family and culture to culture. These patterns and styles may or may not have been functional for the family in the past. What needs to be determined in the assessment is how well the usual communication patterns are working in the current situation and life stage.

It is helpful for the clinician to think in terms of congruence versus incongruence when seeking to understand the effectiveness of communication between older and younger family members. Congruence refers to the ability to give a consistent message; for example, to say what one means and mean what one says. Thoughts, feelings, and behavior match. The case example cited above of the daughter and mother who censored their communication so as not to say anything upsetting typifies incongruent communication. In this case, as in so many others, such rules of communication can prove to be detrimental to the well-being of all family members. Miscommunication precludes revealing needs and emotions in ways that elicit clear responses.

Assessment needs to examine the extent to which rules and styles of communication have kept pace with the evolution and needs of the family. What is acceptable communication between parents and children must evolve as people develop and age. The entire assessment process should reveal the strengths and problems of communication in the family as family members assemble together to talk about the current situation. This meeting is an opportunity not only to understand communication processes, but also to begin to change them if needed.

One reason that communication problems between older adults and their families are so frequent is that the family members believe they have so many fearsome things to talk about. Clinicians who work with this population find it rare for families to discuss dependency, fears of the future, death, needs, and desires. Each generation is reluctant to engage in these conversations. Such discourse is painful; members fear that open discussions will raise distressing issues from the past. Assessment must center on understanding the nature and style of communication, what needs to be communicated, and what interferes with effective communication.

THE SOCIO-CULTURAL EDGE

Throughout this chapter, we have noted that a family's way of being a family and of dealing with relationships between generations is dependent to a large extent upon ethnic heritage and identity. The therapist must take this factor into account when assessing a family, its concerns, and possible resolutions of those concerns. It is at this edge that the therapist must operate, using a resource model of family functioning as suggested early in this chapter. The practitioner consequently will not view the older client and his or her family through a lens of standard norms by which to measure strengths and weaknesses. The resource model leads the clinician to assume that the family is "continually generating its own norms in an interacting context of history, culture, ethnicity, social class, politics, interpersonal relationships, and individual quirks" (Imber-Black, 1986, p. 149). This attitude of welcoming diversity and a willingness to interpret differences as strengths sets the tone for assessment and the ongoing helping process.

Ecomap

A most important edge to be addressed with older adults and their families is the relationship between the family and the community or larger society. The nature and quality of these relationships will often be critical for the family's success in getting its needs met. Many problems are actually the result of inadequate or stressful connections with organizations in the extended environment of the family. A tool useful for assessing a family's connections with the external environment is the ecomap. This instrument is a diagram of the family in its relationship with the various external resources. A sample ecomap of the Berry family from Chapter 1 is presented in Appendix C. Many practitioners are familiar with this tool. For those who are not, we provide a brief summary of the procedures and the process.

Designing an ecomap involves placing the members of the household within a large circle that marks the boundary between the family and its external environment. The household members and their relationships are mapped by the same symbols as those used for the genogram. The large circle is surrounded by smaller circles, which represent the external systems to which the family is or could be connected. Connecting lines indicate the nature and the quality of these relationships. A solid line indicates a strong connection; a dotted line indicates a tenuous connection. Slash marks along either line designate a conflictual or stressful relationship. Varying experiences of each family member are shown by separate lines between the individual and the community organizations or systems. Descriptive words elicited from the family further illuminate the emerging ecological picture of the family and its members.

The ecomap is an indispensable part of the assessment of older adults and their families. A completed map yields a picture of connections or lack of them to friends, neighbors, extended family, religious institutions, health services, recreational facilities, transportation, and many other external resources. It pinpoints areas of satisfaction and tension. The ecomap can also be constructed to assess change over time. An ecomap of the situation "then" is compared to one drawn to reveal "now."

The ecomap is another technique to involve family members as full participants in the assessment process. The practitioner may guide the procedure, but it is the family members who perform the actual work. They tell their story about how they relate to the outside world, and whether they find these interactions stressful or comfortable. The sociocultural reality of the family from their point of view emerges in this picture of resources and unmet needs. The therapist and the family can then define what interventions in the larger society will be needed. Some families are strengthened by recognizing the resources that they already have in place. Others will need assistance in locating needed resources, activating dormant ones, and/or learning how to communicate effectively with outside organizations.

SUMMARY

This chapter has focused on the problems, processes, and procedures that constitute a family assessment of older adults and their families. We have emphasized a collaborative and empowering approach to assessment and have suggested some techniques and guidelines for the practitioner. The next chapter presents a framework for treatment based upon such an assessment.

EXERCISES

1. Construct a genogram for your family of origin. What are the intergenerational patterns for caretaking of the elderly? How do these patterns fit the feelings and attitudes of caretaking in your present generation?

2. How is seeking help outside the family viewed by members of your family of origin? How does your ethnic heritage support and/or hinder your seeking help outside the family for an elderly member?

3. Devise several questions that would help you understand the meaning of seeking help from sources outside the family. Try them out with your own family or with the family of a friend.

4. Have a conversation with your siblings about how each of you should be involved in taking care of your parents if the need arises.

5. Interview someone you know who participates in the care of an elderly parent. Focus on how the caring activities have changed the life and relationships of the caretaking person.

6. Ask extended family and friends for stories about difficulties in family communication that have interfered with an elderly person's receiving needed care.

7. Assess either your own family or another family in terms of structure and communication. Focus on what changes have occurred as the older generation aged. Try to find examples of outmoded patterns. Try to discover what changes would facilitate healthier relationships between the older and middle generations. What feedback do you think would be helpful to the family for initiating needed changes?

Chapter 4

A FRAMEWORK FOR TREATMENT

As a preparation to exploring specific issues of aging and the involvement of the families of the elderly in their treatment, we first delineate some fundamental components of family treatment. This chapter begins with a reminder to "think family." We then present some of the major interventions used in family treatment. The chapter concludes with a section on culture, an important ingredient in many instances of family therapy with the elderly.

THINKING FAMILY

In preceding chapters, we stressed the need to "think family" when providing services to older adults. Family relations involving elder members are often hidden. Older people are more likely to present somatic symptoms than emotional ones, and to approach medical personnel rather than psychiatric or mental health professionals. Emotional features may not be detected in medical examinations or may be attributed solely to organic conditions without considering the role of the family in exacerbating or relieving those symptoms. Walsh (1982) points to the "vicious cycle of family overfunctioning/patient underfunctioning [that] can hasten and perpetuate symptoms labeled as 'senility' " (p. 215).

The not infrequent claim of older adults that they have no family may mistakenly be taken at face value. On the other hand, "intimacy at a distance" (Walsh, 1980, p. 215) is a prevalent pattern that compels providers to assess relationships beyond who is sharing the current household. We conclude by reminding the clinician that when younger family members present themselves or their children for assistance, problems involving elder members may be an important part of the system. Thinking family also requires being aware of one's own attitudes about the elderly and aging. This may help minimize possibilities of depersonalizing older adults and inadvertently adopting attitudes that elders are a poor investment for therapy, are too resistant to change, or simply are untreatable. These caveats were explored in more detail in Chapter 2.

INTERVENTIONS FOR CHANGE

After a complete assessment that includes not only early family history but also current relationships and recent changes within the family and for the individual, it is time to address how to effect change. The assessment process itself is a potent tool for change. Genograms point out family expectations for roles and rules. Members begin to recognize patterns and significant forces within the family system as a history is taken. Although the concept of change may seem elusive to family members, once new understanding has occurred through the assessment process, change has already begun.

General principles for family treatment with older adults encompass the following goals: directing interventions at attempted solutions to the problem; enhancing the level of functioning and the independence of the older adult, but not at the expense of other family members; and using the least amount of intervention possible.

Types of Interventions

Interventions within the discipline of family therapy are varied, as are their uses. It is helpful to categorize interventions as direct or indirect. This classification is related to the previously noted conceptualization of change as first order or second order. (For further explanation and illustrations of this theory of change, see Chapter 2, the section on reframing the problem.) Briefly, first-order change is one in which the system is not changed; second-order change involves change within the system itself. Direct interventions are those aimed at first-order change. They evoke a response of compliance on the part of family members. Indirect interventions, on the other hand, are inferential and consist of implied or conflicting messages that differ in the amount of clarity and directness. They are received with a corresponding variation in client awareness of the message. These latter interventions, to be considered when first-order change appears to be inadequate, are aimed at second-order change.

Direct interventions have as their purpose the solution of immediate problems and a decrease in levels of stress. Through these interventions, the clinician negotiates with the family their meaning of the problem. The process unfolds as follows: The therapist brings new information to the family members, who then absorb or process that information in their own way. They feed their interpretation of the information back to the therapist. This new information from the family may change the therapist's view of the family's situation, thereby enabling the therapist to become more helpful. Direct interventions are more effective when the family members are accepting in their response to the posing of a practical or commonsense type of solution to the family's problem. Direct interventions usually represent the least amount of intervention. Examples of direct interventions include but are not limited to the following:

Redesign of the family structure
Provision of information the family lacks
Family guidance in use of reminiscence or life review
Interpretation of the family genogram
Encouragement of new ways to communicate
Eliciting new information via circular questioning
Renegotiating boundaries and tasks of the life stage
Coaching alternate behavioral responses
Advocating for the family and establishing a network within the community

The use of indirect interventions is considered for several reasons. The family may not be able to utilize the clinician's expertise. Perhaps direct interventions do not alter basic family processes. Or family members may wish to change the general direction of their lives. For example, a couple learned how to communicate using appropriate communication techniques, yet the wife complained that the marriage was "work" and seemed dreary. Another example is that of an older mother who fulfilled all the demands of her adult daughter, who nevertheless continued to fret about feeling unloved. Whatever the reason for the clinician's use of an indirect intervention, it is not to resolve an immediate problem per se. The delivery of indirect interventions may take different forms. For example, a single intervention is directed toward a particular family member; or several or all family members are given related indirect assignments; or the focus becomes a system of behavior or relationships between and among family members. These types are listed in the order of increasing complexity.

The essence of an indirect intervention is that the result of its being followed will be the opposite of what it is seemingly intended to accomplish. Its success depends on the family defying the therapist's instructions, or adhering to them to the point of absurdity and then refusing compliance. The target of the intervention must be a symptom or problematic behavior that is related to a dysfunctional aspect of the family system. The dysfunction could be a secret alliance, contest, or coalition that the family is reluctant to reveal or change.

Examples of indirect interventions include but are not limited to the following:

Eliciting new information via circular questioning

Positive connotation and reframing of problematic behavior

Re-storying

Assignment of ordeals, transition rituals, or other homework tasks

Restraining change

Use of the direct and indirect interventions listed above will be illustrated throughout the next two chapters as we examine the need for family work when addressing various problems and issues of aging. Some of the interventions, however, warrant preliminary explication.

Reminiscence and Life Review

Reminiscence is a remembering of the past. It is "a way of reliving, re-experiencing or savoring events of the past that are personally significant" (Silverman, Brahce, & Zielinski, 1981, p. 217). It places one's life in perspective by seeing oneself as a whole in relation to time, in relation to both the external and the internal worlds, in relation to self and others. Reminiscence is often accompanied by feelings of nostalgia, regret, and pleasure.

Workers need to be aware of a misconception that, because older adults exhibit a tendency toward self-reflection and reminiscence, these processes are indicative of loss of recent memory and therefore of decline. Many elders' great need to talk can be experienced as boring by workers or family members. Fortunately the positive value of reminiscence is now more widely understood, although this view is also tempered with a realistic acknowledgment of the risks involved.

Among the assets of reminiscence for the older person are the means to:

Maintain self-esteem and reinforce a sense of identity

Feel a sense of achievement and pleasure

Cope with stresses related to the aging process

Gain status by revealing selected elements of his or her life history

Place both positive and negative aspects of the past in perspective

Deal with emotions such as grief

Establish a common ground for communication
            (Silverman, Brahce, & Zielinski, 1981, p. 217)

Grief and other powerful feelings may be activated by the process of reminiscence. These feelings should be validated as relevant and not be glossed over hastily in a well-meaning but patronizing reassurance. Guilt is a significant emotion for clients of any age and warrants the curative components of therapy.

The common ground listed as the last item above is salient for family therapy. The elder's reminiscence is a vehicle for other family members to become recipients of a sense of the family history. Members also can participate in a rich opportunity to understand the older person better by means of this mutual sharing of information and experiences. Family myths can be addressed with a greater appreciation and acknowledgment of each member's particular reality. The following case illustrates the use of reminiscence.

Ever since Mr. Solomon died, his widow declined in health. She began calling on their daughter to make the hour's drive to her home, sometimes in the middle of the night, whenever her emphysema flared up enough to inhibit her breathing. As a result, the daughter and mother agreed that Mrs. Solomon should move to a retirement complex located closer to the daughter. However, the mother then became increasingly estranged from her close friends and neighbors. They were elderly like herself, and Mrs. Solomon was reluctant to take the initiative to invite them for visits that entailed the long drive. At this point Mrs. Solomon's daughter realized that the situation was getting out of hand and sought counseling for herself and her mother. The therapist encouraged Mrs. Solomon through reminiscence to identify early patterns of expecting little for herself unless she was in crisis. It became clear that in childhood her parents had been busy managing their restaurant, and her older siblings as teenagers had often been occupied with their own pursuits. She was left to fend for herself although help was available for dire needs. Family counseling enabled the mother and daughter to arrange for alternatives for Mrs. Solomon's care that set limits on appeals to the daughter and yet confirmed the availability of family support. Mrs. Solomon slowly developed a group of friends at the retirement center. As her needs for her daughter's reassurance diminished, so did the frequency of the attacks of emphysema. The practitioner employed the intervention of reminiscence at various times throughout the course of therapy, first to reveal dysfunctional early patterns of coping, but later to build Mrs. Solomon's awareness of her strengths and successes, and to resolve her guilt stemming from her choice of mate in marriage.

In contrast to reminiscence, life review usually refers to an organized inventory of one's life, which is more than a simple recall of the past. Life review may include activities such as studying a family album or scrapbooks or other memoirs, exploring the family genealogy, or making pilgrimages to places of past significance. Robert Butler, one of the first to propose the use of life review and reminiscence as positive tools for work with the elderly, developed a comprehensive Life Review Form for those who wish a structured format for the collection of this information (Butler & Lewis, 1982, pp. 205-224).

The life review should not be limited to the elder's autobiography. Instead information should be gathered from other family members as well. Life review is employed as an intervention with goals of reconciling family rifts, passing values and information to other generations, enhancing creativity in seeking solutions to problems, facilitating the process of mourning, or resolving individual intrapsychic conflicts and guilt. Life review as a part of family therapy can adjust or abort dysfunctional, repetitive patterns of behaviors and attitudes. Butler and Lewis (1982) list the results of resolution through life review as atonement, serenity, constructive reorganization, and creativity.

The debate continues as to the risks of reminiscence and life review. Butler and Lewis (1982) refer to possible untoward effects and cite

extreme emotional pain in the form of guilt, despair, obsessive rumina-
tion, panic, and even suicide. Hughston and Cooledge (1989), in their
examination of research on life review, report a finding that reminiscence reduces negative affect more than it increases the positive affect.
In addition it appears that depressed clients, in contrast to more lively
ones, spontaneously focus less upon the past and with more difficulty;
likewise, their reminiscence is apt to attend to negative events. The
reviewers conclude that because of the "lack of precision in ability to
predict outcomes of a reminiscence experience, therapists who choose
to utilize techniques that maximize reflection upon the past should do so
with knowledge of risk taking and respect for the unknown" (Hughston &
Cooledge, 1989, p. 50).

The above reviewers note conclusions from research indicating that
middle-aged adults utilize reminiscence more for problem solving than
do elders whose purpose is more for personal life satisfaction. They
point to the significant range of efficacy in the use of reminiscence and
life review as tools in intergenerational clinical work.

Circular Questioning

Whereas reminiscence and life review are interventions accepted
historically for use in both individual and family approaches to treatment with the elderly, circular questioning is a development in the field
of family therapy and is applicable primarily to work with family
systems. Its roots extend back to early studies of cybernetics and family
systems in the 1970s. Then, in Milan, Selvini Palazzoli, Boscolo,
Cecchin, and Prata (1980) introduced the therapeutic tool of circular
questioning as a clarification of their methods of indirect interventions.

Circular questioning is a type of systemic investigation of family
members during a family session. Each member of the family, in turn,
is asked his or her view of a specific aspect of the family functioning.
The aspect could be the family problem in general, the history of the
problem, a sequence of behaviors, an unspoken issue, the thoughts/feel-
ings/values/meanings of behaviors of other family member(s), or other
issues needing identification, examination, or intervention. Some examples of circular questioning are: Who agrees with you that this is the
problem? When your daughter and son are fighting, what does your
grandson do? What does it mean to you that day after day nothing
between you and your daughter changes? Who is most like you of your

four children? How does grandfather's behavior bother you differently than it does other family members?

Utilization of this therapeutic tool has as its goal the family's increased awareness of the reciprocal interrelatedness of behaviors. Circular questioning challenges the family's static truths, which are evinced by phrases such as "Grandmother *is* old-fashioned" or "My husband *is* stingy." Circular questioning uses the language of relationships, not of "what is" (Cecchin, 1987, p. 412). Circular questioning is in itself a vehicle for change.

A dramatic example of how circular questioning leads to change occurred during a session with the Berry family discussed in Chapter 1. At one point, Mr. Berry commented that a major reason for his retirement was to take care of Mrs. Berry. He felt that if he were to spend more time with her, she would be busier and less depressed. The option to continue teaching was open to him but he decided Mrs. Berry's welfare was more important. The following is an excerpt from the discussion that followed Mr. Berry's comments:

Therapist: Who else in the family knew of John's reason for retirement?

Mrs. Berry: Well, he told me that he would retire if it would help me. But I said that it was not necessary. I knew how much he loved his teaching and his plays.

Barbara: I never knew for sure why Dad retired when he didn't really need to. I do remember that he once told me "Your mother needs me at home."

Steven: Dad always said that he retired for Mom. But I don't really think that was the whole reason.

Mr. Berry: What do you mean?

Steven: Well, don't you remember that you were getting unhappy about how the students seemed to be changing? You felt they were harder to control and less respectful. You said once that they were criticizing your teaching.

Therapist: Who agrees with Steven's idea about the retirement?

Mr. Berry: There is some truth to it. Things were changing. Teaching was not as satisfying. Yes, it wasn't all for Martha.

Mrs. Berry: I always thought there was more to it but did not want to say so.

Barbara: So that was it. I thought it was great of you to want to help
Mom but I really never believed that she needed you to give
up your work. Now it makes sense.

Thus two circular questions focused upon eliciting the family's
understanding of how the retirement triggered change in this family. Mrs.
Berry's position as the "patient" for whom her husband was sacrificing was
modified. Mr. Berry was also revealed to be experiencing some problems.
Premises about Mr. Berry as the "strong" one and Mrs. Berry as the "weak"
one were now open for questions and discussion.

The Milan group (Selvini Palazzoli et al., 1980) introduced circular
questioning as a technique that promotes and supports the practitioner's
hypothesizing, circularity, and neutrality when interviewing families.
They define hypothesizing as "the formulation by the therapist of an
hypothesis based upon the information he possesses regarding the
family he is interviewing. The hypothesis establishes a starting point
for his investigation as well as his verification of the validity of this
hypothesis" (p. 4). Circularity is defined as "the capacity of the therapist
to conduct his investigation on the basis of feedback from the family in
response to the information he solicits about relationships and, therefore,
about difference and change" (1980, p. 8). And neutrality refers to the
effect of the clinician's behavior on the family during the session:

> As long as the therapist invites one member to comment upon the rela-
> tionship of two other members, he appears *at that time* to be allied to that
> person. However, this alliance shifts the moment he asks *another* family
> member and yet another to do the same. The end result of the successive
> alliances is that the therapist is allied with everyone and no one at the same
> time. (1980, p. 11)

Neutrality provides the context for building hypotheses, which in
turn provide a context for seeing circular patterns and asking circular
questions. Circular questioning is an intervention requiring clinical
creativity that is enhanced by curiosity.

Fleuridas, Nelson, and Rosenthal (1986) examine in detail the various
aspects of circular questioning as a tool for assessment and treatment. They
first describe the circular interview in terms of the Milan group's concepts
of neutrality, hypothesizing, and circularity, plus intervention. They then
present a comprehensive classification and summary of uses of circular
questioning, which include the following:

Problem definition

Obtaining a sequence of interactions

Comparison/classification of relationships, beliefs, values, myths, thoughts, and feelings

Identification of differences, changes, agreements/disagreements, explanations/meanings

Dimensions of time: past, present, or future/hypothetical

Finally several pages are devoted to practical examples of the different types of questions, each of which can be adapted easily to family therapy with the elderly. This is an informative and comprehensive reference for those human service providers wishing to develop skills in the use of circular questioning.

Family members may resist answering any explanation-seeking questions, including circular questions. Clients may be reluctant to reveal their lack of information, may fear giving inaccurate information, may wish to avoid blaming others, and may predict consequences of retribution for revealing family secrets. Furman and Ahola (1988) suggest several tactics for averting such opposition. The clinician could explain that the intention is not to obtain the "right" answer but instead to enhance the clinician's understanding of the various ways of thinking that family members have used in their attempts to explain the problem. Or the question could be reformulated, that is, repeated in a new way. If a family member responds with "I don't know" to the question of Who is most concerned when you are feeling ill?, the therapist might then ask, Who has time to call you when you are ill? Other strategies to handle client reluctance to answering the questions might be to "use their imagination," to offer various alternatives from which the members might choose, or to "gossip in their presence." This last technique, related to circular questioning, involves asking family members their impressions of other people's explanations, rather than giving their own. One member, upon hearing the interpretation of his view by another member, might feel compelled to correct that statement and thus reveal his own explanation.

Although we have listed circular questioning as an example of direct intervention, it is also used in an indirect fashion to dispel myths, challenge rigid thinking, make overt what has been covert, and abort dysfunctional patterns. When thus applied, the element of neutrality of circular questioning is more difficult to maintain, and hypothesizing may or may not remain a principal focus.

The questions that were asked of the Berry family in the session described earlier in the chapter were indirect interventions challenging the family's premise of Martha as the problematic member. An element of hypothesizing also took place in this example of circular questioning, which occurred relatively early in treatment; the extent of the family's rigidity was assessed as their fixed meaning was confronted.

Reframing the Behavior or Situation

Reframing is an indirect intervention that effects second-order change. It is the process of giving a particular situation or behavior a different meaning. Reframing brings a new view or reality, which "challenges the family's construction of events and behavior, offering a new context for understanding and thus stimulating altered responses and new options" (Hartman & Laird, 1983, p. 309).

We have already addressed reframing in terms of making the problem a solvable one. We discussed in some detail in Chapter 2 the concept of reframing as part of the preparatory stage of family treatment. Reframing is also the foundation of many of the indirect strategies such as positive connotation and can be used in conjunction with the intervention of restraining a symptom or change.

An example of reframing used as an indirect intervention is positive connotation or labeling, that is, giving a negative behavior a positive meaning. This allows the client and other family members to change their perspective of the behavior while also changing the family's relationship to the behavior. The fixed state of the system that maintains the symptom or behavior is thus disrupted. For instance, a depressed wife might be relabeled as being caringly sacrificial in giving her newly retired spouse a way to feel important and needed as he assumes the household tasks that previously were her responsibility. Other examples are describing withdrawal as taking care of oneself, or crying as being able to express feelings, or confusion as preparation for new growth. As a means of reducing its reluctance to engage in treatment, a family might be told that it is only a strong family that seeks help.

Re-storying

This intervention consists of an individual, or a family in toto, relating their story as a type of metaphor. Change evolves as members reveal the feelings, meanings, and experiences that have led to their thoughts and behaviors. The therapist elicits the meanings that the family has attached to its historical mileposts. Family members examine and begin to understand how these meanings have become obstacles to a higher level of functioning and a goodness-of-fit. The family then rewrites its own story, using altered meanings that serve as building blocks for future higher functioning. The following case illustrates the use of re-storying.

A single mother, Mrs. Scott, who had divorced an abusive husband, entered counseling plagued with self-doubt about her competence as a parent and the "rightness" of her decision to divorce. By all external measures, Mrs. Scott was quite successful in a new job and as a mother to her 3-year old son. Her feelings were being fueled by a family belief system that divorce is immoral and that a woman is responsible for making a relationship work. Throughout the divorce process, Mrs. Scott thought that her mother was sympathizing with her spouse while being extremely critical of her. Both parents reminded her that she would not be able to provide financially or emotionally for her young son as he grew older. In the exploration of therapy, Mrs. Scott realized how the story of her gender was restricting her life and her development as an adult. In sessions with her mother, her mother's "story" of wife and mother was explored. Mrs. Scott discovered that her mother had stayed in a very unhappy marriage "for the sake of the children." Mrs. Scott also learned that her mother, too, had secretly resented a belief system that required her to forgo her own desires and needs. The mother had grown up at a time when strong societal norms dictated that successful wives were submissive to their husbands' needs. In that context, Mrs. Scott understood how her decisions to "go it alone" were problematic for her mother and were adding to the mother's sense of loss about her own dreams and aspirations. Not only did this realization strengthen the relationship between the two women, but it also helped each to change her self-image. Mrs. Scott then was able to speak of her decision to leave her husband as "courageous" and to acknowledge her own subsequent successes. The therapist posed to each family member the question, If you continue to think of yourself in these new ways, how do you think the story of your future will go? Having already begun to reclaim her life from a dysfunctional "story," Mrs. Scott was ready to go on to "reauthor" a more satisfying future life story. This process entailed the development of a healthier family story that supported the needs of all members. Mrs. Scott's parents entered marital counseling.

The intervention of re-storying entails a metaphorical reframing of past events. The reframing includes the use of positive connotation as the family learns what external or   forces led to the development of the problematic meanings. Guilt is thus allayed.

Prescribing a Ritual or Ordeal

This indirect intervention consists of the clinician telling the family member(s) to do more of what they are already doing that creates and perpetuates the problematic behavior. A behavior is to be made longer or stronger, or made into an ordeal. For instance, a family that is quarreling frequently is told to quarrel at least every day for 10 minutes before breakfast, 10 minutes before dinner, and at 9:30 at night for 10 minutes. An underlying premise for the use of this strategy is that if the symptom is made more difficult to maintain than to give up, the symptom will be relinquished. Or perhaps the absurdity of the exaggerated situation will become obvious.

One goal of this type of intervention is the family's greater awareness of having choices. Another is an increase in family members' attention to each other's particular, distinct behavior. And an important advantage of this strategy is that the family is allowed to give up its dysfunctional behavior slowly or at its own pace. Resistance to the undesirable behavior lessens, and so does the sense of hopelessness when the behavior recurs.

A word of warning. Behaviors physically dangerous to self or others should not be prescribed unless a deep clinical understanding of the family dynamics is firmly in place and the clinician is highly skilled in the delivery of indirect interventions. Even then it is usually wise to seek an alternative method for promoting second-order change.

Restraining Change

Restraining change means telling the family or its members not to change a problematic behavior, or not to change at all. Assuming the symptom or problem is an integral part of the family system, the family is restrained from change. As the family members react to this instruction and press for change, the therapist carefully regulates their rate of change by predicting difficulties if the change occurs or is too rapid. The heart of this intervention is the matching of therapeutic efforts to effect change with the family's natural pace of functioning. This intervention is indirect in nature; it thus directs second-order change.

The clinician restraining the problematic behavior or change might refer to doubts about the consequences of change, doubts that the family could handle the happy state of having no arguments that they cite as their goal. Or members of another family might be warned that their obsessive attention to the grandmother's activities should continue for a while because the adult daughter is not ready to address her dissatisfaction in her marriage with her husband.

Summary

The interventions we have chosen to highlight are some that have withstood the test of time. As the field of family therapy continues to evolve, however, new insights and understandings will ensue. The alert clinician will become aware of new interventions as they are designed and recognized, and as their applications are examined.

ETHNICITY—GENDER—CULTURE

Most contemporary human service providers agree that social relations are an essential ingredient in the complex process called "aging well." From birth to death, we are shaped by our surroundings, by our social environment, and by our families, all of which also evolve over time. The family passes through stages of the life cycle: the stage of couples, to that of new parents with young children, then to parents with adult children beginning their own families, to parents with adult children and grandchildren, and finally to the now more common stage of elderly parents with aging children who themselves are grandparents. These developmental experiences do not occur in a social vacuum but interact with the ethnic, racial, or cultural context of society within which family members live. Antonucci and Akiyama (1991) have studied at length the interplay between aging and social relations, and comment upon the overlay of ethnic factors:

> The lives of Italian Americans, African Americans, or Asian Americans are likely to be quite different in a variety of areas, from food and dress to expected forms of family interactions and cultural or religious rituals. Each of these lends a distinct flavor to all the interactions and social relations of the individual, regardless of other important determining characteristics such as socioeconomic status, education, and geographic differences. (p. 40)

Factors of ethnicity, gender, and culture are of utmost importance to the human service provider, who is obliged not only to become aware of the characteristics of these elements, but also to become adept at including them in the planning and delivery of treatment. Therefore this chapter concludes with highlights of factors salient for treatment that are sensitive to ethnicity, gender, and culture.

Sensitivity to Ethnicity

Whereas service to older adults by community mental health centers increased markedly in some states in the mid-1980s, service to elderly minorities increased at a much slower rate:

> In nearly all comparisons (number of staff and percent of elderly served, appropriateness of services and their acceptance by older adults, placement of elderly in state hospitals and in nursing homes), minorities did not experience improvements in service comparable to those available to older adults in general. This is especially worrisome because they started in a more disadvantaged position. (Powell & Fellin, 1987, p. 11)

It is clear that explicit needs of minorities must be recognized both in the design of programs and in the details of their delivery.

Guidelines to Ethnicity

A framework can be helpful for understanding and possibly predicting the extent to which traditional ethnic patterns will surface in a particular family (McGoldrick, 1982, p. 402). Some aspects to be explored include why the family immigrated and what it was seeking and leaving, such as religious or political persecution, poverty, or even adventure. How long has it been since the first family members immigrated, and since the last members came to this county? Did the family come together or over a period of time? Does the family live in an ethnic neighborhood? What are the socioeconomic status, education, and upward mobility of the family members? How intact are religious and political allegiances and contacts with the ethnic group? What is the family's attitude toward its ethnic group? What languages are spoken by which family members? Has there been intermarriage outside the ethnic group or have other connections been made with other ethnic groups? These questions of ethnic origin, asked of any family, will provide a foundation and framework for treatment.

More specific guidelines and warnings for appropriate delivery of services to minority older adults and their families begin with the statement that much diversity occurs within each minority group, and this increases in relation to the period of time of residence in the adopted country. Elder members who were born in this country or members who arrived here at an early age are likely to support family roles that have been influenced by their years in the American workplace. Their family patterns as a result tend to be more egalitarian than those of families whose elders are recent arrivals. When interacting with families who maintain the strong hierarchical structure of earlier generations in another country, perhaps because elder members are still rooted in their old family ways, the clinician should be aware of the need to respect this structure.

An example is the family session in which translation to the ethnic language is needed for older family members to comprehend the transactions. Clearly it is important for all members to participate in the treatment in some fashion. Yet if a child or young adult member more fluent in English is asked to interpret for an elder member, this can reverse inappropriately the vertical hierarchical structure of many ethnic minority families, especially Hispanic or Asian-American ones (Ho, 1987). It is better to request an adult, external interpreter for such situations. If a bilingual professional is not accessible, an adult, non-family, bilingual member of the ethnic group can be chosen as long as the person's objectivity is assured. Assuming that the parents are ready to be interviewed with their children, an assumption not to be reached lightly, one option is to address the older generation in their native language and the children in English. This interaction strengthens intergenerational boundaries, but of course necessitates a bilingual therapist.

Respect for Hierarchy

Children learn the language of the new country and become acculturated more rapidly than elder family members. Authoritarian parents or grandparents dependent upon them for translation with people who are community resources may feel threatened. Family therapists need to recognize the impact of immigration, political discrimination, and cultural adjustment upon their clients of ethnic heritage. Clinicians should offer services of mediation and cultural translation in addition to the more usual aspects of treatment. They should also pay special attention

to joining with these families in the early phase of therapy to minimize
whatever potential there may be for distrust from past difficulties with
authorities at the time of immigration and settlement.

Ethnic Culture

Respect for hierarchy is only one element that deserves attention in
the treatment of ethnic minority families. Ho (1987) refers to studies
that indicate that " 'successful' or 'acculturated' ethnic minority families show a strong interest and need in keeping alive the folkways, arts
and crafts, language, and values associated with their heritage" (p. 19).
For instance the usual American clinician views "mastery over nature"
as the mode for effecting change that may conflict with the mode of
"being in nature," the predominant stance of some ethnic groups. The
clinician must learn therefore how the family perceives change, not only
in what can be changed but also how, when, and by whom. Mainstream
America's preferred mode of activity, that of "doing," implies competition and upward mobility. For some ethnic groups, however, including
Asian/Pacific Americans and African-Americans, "doing" means self-
discipline and endurance. Native Americans and Hispanic Americans,
on the other hand, value being more than doing. These differences have
important implications for treatment. A family member of a "being-ori-
ented" ethnic group may be especially sensitive to showing and receiving respect, and may feel insulted if this interactional element is not
behaviorally manifest in the treatment process.

This factor was expressed poignantly at a recent intake appointment.
A female counselor was leading an Asian family to the therapy room.
Unaware that the family's culture prescribed that adult males walk
before women, the faster the father walked to try to take the lead, the
faster the counselor walked. The result was a breathless counselor and
an affronted client, who took his family from treatment.

Such situations underscore the need for an awareness of the client's
cultural customs. And as always, the general clinical principle of respect for the client's rights of self-determination and noninterference
should be kept in mind. Treatment at the minimal level of intrusion is
indicated.

Aspects of Time

Ethnic groups vary also in terms of time orientation. Mainstream
American culture is future-oriented, supportive of sacrifice for future

gains, and worshipful of youth. Native Americans, however, focus upon rhythms of the present. And Asian-Americans revere the past and their ancestors, which symbolize for them both respectability and wisdom. Hispanics have a strong tradition of hierarchy, which emphasizes the past, but also includes a significant element of individuality. African-Americans who have a family history of slavery tend to focus upon the present and try to forget some of the past. Generally ethnic minorities are more amenable to present, concrete approaches than to those which are more abstract, philosophical, or future-oriented (Ho, 1987). Forms of family therapy that are structural, behavioral, and pragmatic are to be given primary consideration for clinical work with ethnic groups. Indirect interventions are usually counterindicated, except for the intervention of reframing, which should be reserved for emphasizing the positive. A Bowenian intergenerational approach is often helpful if it is not too intellectual and lengthy a form of therapy.

Relationship to Others

Another dimension useful for the identification of ethnic characteristics is the relationship with others. Mainstream Americans are more likely to be individualistic and to emphasize autonomy and competition, whereas ethnic groups prefer collectivity. Children of ethnic groups therefore may be incorrectly assessed as "unmotivated" and adult members as "lazy" or "unproductive" when they are reluctant to compete at work or play. However, these families' significant capabilities for cooperation can be mobilized for problem solving in family sessions.

Transferring children from one nuclear family to another within an extended family system is another example of how groups vary in relationships with others. This practice, uncommon in the predominant American culture, is a frequent occurrence with ethnic minorities. It should not be considered dysfunctional unless it has created a problem such as unclear expectations for roles and behaviors. One consistent feature of ethnic families is the involvement of the extended family, especially the grandparents and other older adults, in the rearing and guidance of children. A strong closeness between a child and grandparents may be more of an indicator of the ethnic culture of the family than of a defective parent-child bond. Extended families of ethnic minorities often include lifelong friends in addition to blood kin and need to be assessed for the involvement of these members for implications for treatment. It is not uncommon for well-meaning but misguided clinicians to struggle in vain to effect change in a family pattern when an influential grandparent or aunt or uncle representing the status quo is not brought into treatment.

Most ethnic minority families consider their extended families to be their primary source of support and an arena that provides a reduction in feelings of humiliation, defeat, and powerlessness. If such a natural support system is not available, the clinician should enlist the aid of a folk healer, priest, or religious leader. At the least, an informed therapist can interpret the family's needs to relevant workers in the community.

Older members of ethnic families tend to oppose ethnic intermarriage within their family system. They fear a weakening of the traditional values and mores, a lessening of the ties with their family and nation of origin. Family clinicians can help the older adult examine the prejudices, fears, and myths historically associated with intermarriage, which increase the young couple's risk of marital failure.

Intergenerational patterns are often specific to certain ethnic groups:

> WASP families are likely to feel they have failed if their children do not move away from the family and become independent . . . while Italian families are likely to feel they have failed if their children do move away. Jewish families will expect a relatively democratic atmosphere to exist in the family, with children free to challenge parents and to discuss their feelings openly. . . . Greek families, in contrast, do not expect or desire open communication between generations and would not appreciate the therapist getting everyone to discuss and "resolve" their conflicts. Children are expected to respect parental authority, which is maintained by the distance parents preserve from their children. . . . Irish families will be embarrassed to share feelings and conflicts across generations and cannot be expected to do so to any great extent. (McGoldrick et al., 1982, p. 20)

As to older family members in particular, native American and Greek grandparents often are assigned the role of child rearing and the parents the role of earning income, as already mentioned. Black elderly members tend to receive support from a wide range of family members, not only those related by blood. With some ethnic groups, such as French-Canadians, aging brings status for both genders: grandmothers are considered the family historians, and the death of this generation can weaken kinship ties. Greek grandparents often are controlling and need to be included in the planning of family treatment, although they may not agree to participate in family sessions. Godparents are significant members of Portuguese families. Jewish grandparents, even if holding generally traditional views, often are more accepting of their grandchildren's intermarriage than are their less traditional adult children who may attribute any disapproval to the grandparents.

McGoldrick and colleagues (1982) summarize ethnic features in relation to the family life cycle:

> Any life cycle transition can trigger ethnic identity conflicts because they put families more in touch with the roots of their family traditions. . . . All situational crises—divorce, illness, job loss, death, retirement—can compound ethnicity conflicts, causing people to lose a sense of who they are. The more a therapist is sensitive to the need to preserve continuities, even in the process of change, the more he or she can help the family to maintain maximum control of its context and build upon it. (p. 20)

The various ethnic minority subgroups tend to share more life experiences with each other than they do with the mainstream American culture (Yee, 1990). Nevertheless there are important differences between them. We have mentioned some of the similarities and differences, adding implications for treatment. Appendix D outlines some of the differences for middle-class white Americans and ethnic minorities in terms of the dimensions of relation to environment, orientation to time, relations with people, preferred mode of activity, and the essential goodness of man.

It is not possible for us to present in this volume a comprehensive description of the ethnic groups' various characteristics and needs, and their treatment. We have highlighted some of the salient features and refer the reader for details to the rapidly proliferating literature on this subject. For those seeking a more in-depth view of family treatment with ethnic minorities, we suggest the writings of several authors who give both a detailed overview of the subject and an accounting of specific ethnicities. Ho (1987) concentrates upon the predominant minority groups in America, those of Native American, African-American, Hispanic, and Asian origins. In their edited volume, McGoldrick and colleagues (1982) address an extensive range of groups. Kubler-Ross (1975) presents a traditional Jewish view of death that incorporates as a central element the role of the family of procreation as well as the role of the community, for both the dying member and the mourning survivor.

As ethnic minority groups continue to increase in number in this country and as their needs become more widely recognized, it behooves the family therapist to keep abreast of the knowledge and understanding that will accompany such developments. Of course no one human service provider can be well versed in the culture of all minority groups. Clinicians, however, have several responsibilities: to become aware of their own areas of ignorance, stemming from lack of experience with certain ethnic factors; to recognize the groups with which they are intimately familiar, and to make their experience accessible to other less-informed clinicians; and to take what steps are available to expand their own professional knowledge as well as their referral network for work with ethnic groups outside their own understanding.

Consideration of Gender

According to Antonucci and Akiyama (1991), the networks of men and women, including the elderly, differ qualitatively and sometimes quantitatively. Women report both giving and receiving more support with more types of people than do men. Men's support is mainly with the spouse, involving less mutual sharing with networks of children, siblings, parents, family, and friends. This of course implies an expectation that the wife will provide her husband's support as well as serve as the link with other family members. It is not surprising that Antonucci and Akiyama inform us that older women are less happy than men when they report more people being close and generous to them. These women experience a greater demand from additional network members than do men.

It is a generally accepted observation that as men and women age, they become more like one another. Beginning most markedly when the children have grown and left home, women exhibit more of their assertive and achievement-oriented qualities, men their nurturing ones. This trend over time may be disrupted when adult children assume the care of family members of one or two older generations.

Gender factors also vary according to socioeconomic status. Antonucci and Akiyama (1991) report that networks of people of lower socioeconomic status are more gender-segregated, include more relatives, and are more intergenerational than are those of their higher-status counterparts. Middle-class networks tend, on the other hand, to contain similar numbers of men and women and to include more friends with the family members; networks are multiple and serve to meet varying needs. The researchers stress that it is difficult to separate what seem to be factors of socioeconomic status from those of ethnicity because ethnic groups tend to correlate with certain socioeconomic groups.

Self-esteem often relates to status. Many elder women lived most of their lives at a time when the lower status attributed to their gender was not questioned in America. They internalized that cultural status into their self-concept and are therefore vulnerable to the continuing negative effects of that experience. Treatment should take into account that history of oppression because of gender. The Scott case presented earlier in this chapter illustrates many of these issues of gender. For example, the mother served as the connection to other family members, and both mother and daughter were struggling with aspects of giving and receiving, assertiveness, independence, and guilt.

Treatment should be respectful of each gender. Human service providers are reminded that what we see in others is greatly influenced by who we are, and our gender is a significant part of the lens through which we view our clients, their world, and their resources.

The Primacy of Culture

Culture is ever with us and within us; it cannot be erased. Clinicians should understand the importance of the cultural setting of the older adult and the family, of the service provider, and of the service delivery system.

Culture embraces aspects of socioeconomic level, neighborhood, religion, education, and occupation, all in addition to ethnicity and gender. Principal factors are norms, dominant values, worldviews, roles, behavioral styles, language, and modes of interacting and problem solving. Types of available services and forms of their delivery are also a product of culture. The impact of culture upon the elderly of ethnic groups consists of the combined effect of the unique ethnic elements plus elements of the majority culture within which they live.

Culture provides the richness that typifies our contemporary setting. We live in a time of increasingly rapid social change and in a part of the world characterized by ethnic diversity. Family structure accordingly is highly varied and in a state of flux. The family therapist faces the challenge of addressing the shifting needs within our culture.

CASE ILLUSTRATION

The following case illustration demonstrates some aspects of family therapy with the elderly that have been the focus of this and earlier chapters. The case study also serves as the basis for some exercises at the end of this chapter.

The Johnson Family

Mark Johnson, age 39, contacted a local family agency to ask for help with his aging parents. Mark was single, a widower of 2 years with no children. He was currently dating a divorced woman with two children. His parents, June and John Johnson, ages 75 and 78, respectively, lived in a nearby suburb of a large midwestern city. Mark's 42-year-old sister, Jackie, lived with her husband and two teenage daughters in a town about 100 miles away. His 45-year-old divorced brother, Tom, lived alone in a city on the West Coast.

The focus of Mark's distress was his concern about health problems exhibited by his parents. He also was uncomfortable about their increasing reliance upon him for help. It seemed that they expected him to be available to meet their social needs, and he was frequently taking them out to dinner. He was becoming resentful about the amount of time and effort he was putting into his relationship with them.

The therapist asked questions to determine more precisely how Mark viewed the problem with his parents and the implications for his own life. Mark's perception was that his parents' calls to him had increased following his mother's brief hospitalization 6 months ago. She had complained of being dizzy and had seemed disoriented, but evaluations were inconclusive. Both parents had minimized the incident. Mark now traced their desire for more contact with him to that occasion. Mark was concerned as well about his mother's frequent lapses of memory. His parents were arguing more than in the past and often tried to engage him as a mediator. And most of all, Mark was feeling alone in the care of his parents. He envisioned a future with increasing demands upon his time. His parents' claims were already affecting his relationship with his female friend. He came for assistance in how to discuss with his siblings his anxieties about the future and how to obtain their involvement in the care of their parents.

The therapist suggested that Mark bring his sister and brother and his parents to a family session. Mark, however, wished to settle some issues with his siblings first. Besides, he said, he needed the assurance of their support before talking to the parents. The prospect of facing his parents alone was frightening. "After all," he said, "I'm the youngest in the family and I need to check out things with Jackie and Tom." His perception of himself as "the baby of the family" was revealed further as he mentioned being unable thus far to talk to his siblings about his concerns because they never took him seriously. He sought the support of an outside expert.

A meeting was arranged to include Mark and Jackie. Tom had said he could not come because of the distance involved, but agreed to attend at a later date. In the session the therapist asked Mark to describe what had brought him to the agency and what he hoped to achieve in this meeting. Mark spoke of his worries about their parents' arguments and the state of their mother's health. He explained that a process had begun that he feared would require him to spend more and more time with his parents. He reminded his sister of his recent losses and his having just pulled his life together. He wanted time and space for his new relationship and for "getting on with his life." He wanted Jackie to formulate a plan that would be fair to both of them.

Jackie became visibly upset as she listened to her brother. She exclaimed that if Mark had just been able to share his concerns earlier, much pain could have been avoided. "You are just like the rest of the family, keeping your feelings to yourself." Jackie told Mark that she thought he had been withdrawing from her ever since his wife died. Her interpretation was that he feared she would try to talk with him about his sadness. "The problem is that I'm the emotional one in the family and people don't feel comfortable with me. You have never let me know how you feel, so how could I know what you want and need?" She added, "We are a small family and Tom left us years ago, so we had better find a way to work this out."

This beginning opened the way for the two siblings to talk of the past and the future. They aired some grievances but also affirmed their mutual desire for a closer, more supportive relationship. Jackie said she was surprised that Mark would think that she would desert him in the caretaking of their parents. She had even thought she would eventually be the one with the caretaker role and was prepared to have the parents live with her at some point if necessary. The clinician suggested that Mark and Jackie consider how best to approach Tom who had, both agreed, disengaged himself from the family. They decided to write him and tell him of this meeting and what it had accomplished. They also agreed to tell him of their sadness about lack of contact with him and their wish for a different relationship with him.

The last question was how to involve their parents in this process. Both Mark and Jackie had trepidations on that score. This was clearly a family with rigid boundaries when it came to revealing openly a need for help. Engaging each other at the feeling level was to be a new experience. With the support of the therapist, Mark and Jackie devised a plan for talking together with their parents about their concerns. They also agreed to inform Tom of their plan as an attempt to engage him in the process. Mark and Jackie were to meet with their parents and then a family session was to be scheduled.

A series of family meetings followed, and Tom made arrangements to attend two of them. The very process of meeting together with the purpose of discussing their concerns had a major impact upon this family. It was against the family rules and was not easy to do. The elder Mr. Johnson was particularly reluctant, saying that he never could understand what was to be gained by "spewing out your worries and feelings." He had been taught that "if you can't solve your own problems, don't expect others to." The clinician recognized the dilemma for the family in these meetings. At one point she even cautioned them to think deeply about whether they wanted to engage in these talks. She pointed out that they were accustomed to protecting themselves and each other from pain by not talking. Painful feelings and topics were bound to come out in talks about the past, present, and future. After a silence, Jackie said, "I'm more afraid of what will happen if we don't talk." That comment resonated through the family and led to the agreement that "things would have to be different" if family members were to help each other in the future.

The family sessions covered a range of topics. Members talked of their present lives and concerns. The elder Johnsons were able to speak of their fears about aging, especially because the hospitalization seemed to hint at what might come soon. Mrs. Johnson revealed her anger and panic over her memory lapses and what they could mean. Both Mr. and Mrs. Johnson were hesitant to pursue an evaluation, fearing a diagnosis of Alzheimer's disease. On the other hand, Mrs. Johnson wanted to know whether any help might be available, no matter what the diagnosis. When asked by the therapist what support they would need in order to seek an evaluation, they requested information about where to go for it. They also asked Jackie to accompany them, which she agreed to do. This conversation led to others in which family members expressed fears about the aging process and what it would mean for all of them. There was pain but there was also relief. The patterns of communication began to evolve in ways that allowed members to be supportive in realistic ways. Members talked of what they thought their limitations were as well as what they were able to do.

Family meetings focused on the past and the future as well as the present. A genogram led to reminiscences and the identification of family strengths. Jackie, Mark, and Tom asked questions and learned more about their parents as individuals. The parents talked of the aging of their own parents and how they had been involved in that process. In each generation the sense was that aging "just happened." It was not to be discussed; it was too upsetting. Both of Mr. Johnson's parents had died relatively young, and he had not felt close to either of them. Mr. Johnson's experiences gave him little to draw on in facing his own aging. Mrs. Johnson's father died at age 55 of a heart attack. Her mother lived until 80, and Mrs. Johnson had been the primary caretaker in her mother's last years. Mrs. Johnson thought aging would not be pleasant but that somehow her children would know what to do. The family sessions helped both elder Johnsons understand that discussions of needs and expectations could be beneficial to everyone. The boundaries and communication processes in this family became more functional.

With the clinician's help, the three siblings in the family explained to their parents important aspects of their lives and personal concerns. The family talked about the death of Mark's wife, something they had not done before. Mark spoke of his loss and his hopes for the future. Jackie described her struggles as a mother of two teenagers and her desires for a career as a teacher. Tom shared his experience of his divorce and his unresolved feelings regarding it. All three siblings talked from time to time about what it had been like to grow up in this family. This step helped the parents recognize each of their children as adult individuals as well as adult children. The discussions also set the stage for sorting out what each thought would be realistic in terms of availability to the parents for needed future assistance.

The process was not always pleasant, and family members did not resolve all their grievances. However, family members were developing an ability to listen to each other regarding hopes for the future. In addition they were creating a process to be used apart from therapy sessions. At one point the therapist asked family members to imagine themselves 2 years hence, to imagine what their own lives would be like and how they would be relating to each other. Many fears and expectations emerged, but hopes were clear too. It became evident at this juncture that these people intended to be present in each other's lives in the future. That in itself was reassuring.

One occurrence of interest in the family sessions was the parents' assertion of their own personal boundaries as a couple. When Mark raised the issue of the parents' arguments, his father said and his mother agreed that "that's our business." They did not want to discuss the matter in front of their children. Mrs. Johnson offered that if they could not handle this issue, they would talk to someone by themselves. Mark's concern about his parents' arguments diminished as he was reassured of receiving support from his sister and brother in this and other matters.

Treatment of this family raised many issues related to the present, past, and future. The family had been organized in a way that prevented its members from meeting the tasks that they faced individually and as a family. The needs of the elderly parents would likely have gone unmet and perhaps unrecognized until some changes in communication and boundaries were made. The evaluation of Mrs. Johnson was not entirely conclusive, but the best-founded diagnosis was that she was in the early stages of Alzheimer's disease. Family sessions were held to help the family address emotional and practical issues arising from that assessment. The family members' abilities to be available and supportive became much greater than before in spite of the devastation of learning this news. Mrs. Johnson began to access community resources, including a support group for those in early stages of Alzheimer's disease. Her husband cautiously assumed an active role in a support group for family members.

EXERCISES

1. Using the above case illustration, identify both direct and indirect interventions that were employed in the treatment. What are some other interventions that could have been used, with whom, and under what conditions? What interventions would you have been sure not to use?

2. Think of examples in your own practice for the appropriate use of reminiscence. How was this intervention used in the treatment of the Johnsons? What are some other ways reminiscence could have been used in this family's treatment?

3. In what situation(s) have you heard the relating of life history by an older person referred to as an aspect of senility? In at least one of

those instances, how would you give the practice of reminiscence a positive "reframe" and use it as a specific tool for change?

4. Would you use the intervention of restraining change with a Hispanic family in which a grandparent is overinvolved in the activities of a grandchild and the child's mother has begun to drink excessively? Explain.

5. List three different direct interventions you have used with clients, preferably families, to effect change. List three situations appropriate for indirect interventions.

6. As a clinician, what are some of your biases toward the other gender? What qualities do you assume of clients of your own gender; of the other gender; of each gender when the client is an older adult? (A suggestion: Begin with the attitudes of significant members of your own family of origin toward each gender, toward each gender of the elderly, and then consider which attitudes you have adopted as your own.)

7. With which ethnic group(s) are you familiar? How can you make this experience of yours available to other less-informed human service providers?

Chapter 5

FAMILY TREATMENT AND COMMON PROBLEMS RELATED TO THE LIFE CYCLE

As stated in the Introduction, this book is designed to introduce family therapy into the practice of gerontology, not to present gerontology in its entirety. Therefore we have selected certain issues and problems related to aging that we believe should be examined in terms of implications for family involvement. Our selection is representative of issues of aging and provides an appropriate context for illustrations of interventions with families having older adult members.

Problems of the elderly fall into several categories (Keller & Bromley, 1989). Problems relate to personal adjustment and adaptability, as they do for anyone. For the elderly, however, the myths of aging often interfere with effective resolution of these problems. Problems also stem from an imbalance between physiology and personality. At times of stress the decline in physical functioning that is associated with the general process of aging may affect the daily activities of older adults. And problems arise from social and family interactions. Changes in social and family roles, retirement, illness, death of friends, and loss of a spouse all hold potentially negative implications for the elderly and their families. Altered living arrangements and diminishing independence may ensue. "Whenever the need arises for adult children to involve themselves in the care of their parent a central issue is the tension between dependence and independence" (Keller & Bromley, 1989, p. 31).

We now examine how family therapy can assist the elderly and their families in relation to specific areas of concern. As a matter of convenience, we have divided the problem areas into those related more specifically to the life cycle and therefore experienced by most elderly and their families, and those not uncommon but not considered to be part of "normal" aging.

In this chapter we address problems associated with the usual family life cycle: retirement, older couples, death, and loss. We also include here the topic of spirituality, that ingredient which can facilitate the graceful accomplishment of the tasks of life and life's later years. The following chapter, Chapter 6, focuses on other difficulties that elders and their families may encounter: family resistance to elders' independence, long-term care, depression and suicide, substance abuse, and elder abuse.

RETIREMENT

The first recognition of the aging process is apt to be the advent of retirement, previously couched in vague and confusing terms. The mastery of retirement is far from clear, however, and requires changes of role, social network, economic base, management of time, and self-image. The change in these factors in turn affects the relationships between spouses and with the children. Although retirement is dramatic, it need not be traumatic. Everyone responds to retirement, but it need not cause a crisis. What determines the extent of crisis is a variety of factors such as the meaning of work and of retirement, whether retirement is planned or not, whether it is viewed more as the end of a process or as a transfer to a new one, and the support of family and others in making the adjustment. The task at this life cycle stage is to obtain ego differentiation from identification with the work role.

Stages of Adjustment

Retirement may be conceptualized as occurring in three stages (Butler & Lewis, 1982). First is the actual day of retirement, accompanied by celebration, perhaps mixed with some degree of sadness or anxiety. This is followed by a period of adjustment, a longer period, when feelings of confusion, uncertainty, and fear about implications for the future are addressed and adjustments are made. Finally the person arrives at a state of accepting and being "retired." Overpreparation, which usually arises from dissatisfaction during earlier years, and underpreparation, a path to a "rude awakening," are not uncommon. A more successful alternative is to live in the present while taking reasonable precautions for the future, but not waiting for some golden age to arrive.

Retirement clearly necessitates a considerable degree of adjustment. For the retirees, especially men, there are losses of meaningful roles and central relationships at work, losses of means of achievement and productivity, and losses of the family role of provider. Whether the retirement is precipitated by a decline in health or a loss of job are factors that directly relate to the level of stress involved. Similarly retirement accompanied by a change in residence and the loss of contact with community, family, and friends markedly increases the component of stress. Women who retire from years of work may adjust to their own retirement more easily if they have maintained the dual role of worker and homemaker. The continuity of being homemaker tends to ameliorate the transition from the work world, and men also benefit to the degree they have been involved in their home life over the years. Women may encounter more stress in relation to the husband's retirement than to their own, in connection with the loss of job-related social and financial status attached to the husband's work. In all cases, retirement entails a shift in priorities, values, goals, and activities.

Contemporary Trends

The phenomenon of early retirement, especially for men, is a significant feature of contemporary life in America. Early retirement, then followed by a second or third career, postpones most of the painful adjustments to a later time, although entering a different job track produces its own stress. And of course the reasons for early retirement play an important part in the entire process. Did early retirement because of a windfall make earnings in the workplace no longer necessary? Or was it a conscious decision to withdraw from job pressures? Were there family concerns that encouraged early retirement, perhaps in order to relocate near an ailing relative needing care?

Variables of economics, health, and age are important factors in decisions by both men and women when considering retirement. Women working into their older years, as well as the declining opportunities for advancement and earnings for both genders, are also factors that impact heavily upon the consideration of retirement. The trend toward shorter work weeks and longer vacations invites a reevaluation of the primacy of work.

Whatever the precipitants to retirement may be, studies (Mohr & Frankfurt, 1988) indicate that the higher the income, the more careful the planning for retirement. Also the greater the satisfaction with one's physical health, the more successful the adjustment to postretirement life. Pre- and postretirement seminars and counseling offered through employment or private sources may be beneficial, especially when the spouse or family is included.

Treatment of Problems of Retirement

Work serves as a means to structure time, control feelings, provide human contact, and regulate the degree of intimacy of that contact. Substitutes for work and a satisfactory new life-style must be found at retirement. Otherwise the retiree, the spouse, and even the extended family may begin to exhibit a wide range of symptoms. Healthy men and women are known to develop headaches, body pains, digestive disorders, depression, insomnia, nightmares, excessive use of alcohol or prescription medications, lethargy, irritability, and guilt from not working. These symptoms may be present in varying degrees and may be only temporary. The family's response to the retirement and also to any subsequent symptoms will play a crucial role in the course of the retiree's adjustment.

It is not unusual for clinicians to diagnose symptoms of depression, paranoia, confusion, and helplessness in older women whose husbands are grappling with adjustments to retirement. These elder women developed their patterns of marital and intimate relationships long before the rise of feminism and a public espousal of symmetrical relationships. They are accustomed to the one-down stance in marriage, which elevates the husband's sense of adequacy.

A symptomatic wife can give a retired husband a new job:

> As they perceive the impending reality of retirement and sense their husband's response of anxiety or depression, these "good wives" dutifully become increasingly unable to function, exhibiting alarming signs of somatic and emotional deterioration. They know well the power of helplessness. Typically their husbands respond with a show of strength, becoming increasingly concerned and protective toward their wives.

Over time, the wives' symptoms continue to grow worse in the face of all the attempts to solve the problem. When physicians or mental health workers inevitably enter the scene, the wives become "resistant patients." If helping professionals fail to understand the underpinning of the couple's real problem, the origin of the crisis brought on by retirement may be obscured. As the wife-as-resistant-patient becomes less and less responsive to treatment, the frustrated mental health professional often begins to offer more and more drastic solutions, such as plans for nursing homes or alternative caretakers. (Mohr & Frankfurt, 1988, pp. 49-50)

This version of a common scenario gives a clear indication of the need for family or couple therapy. Interventions to reframe or restrain change are often useful in the treatment of such issues. (As we mentioned when discussing interventions in Chapter 6, however, the technique of restraining change is not to be used if there is a risk of suicide.) We already referred to the "helpful wife syndrome" in our presentation of reframing in Chapter 6. And the full case study of the Berry family in Chapter 1 provides an example of treatment of a family that displayed features of a suicidal wife, excessive drinking, threatened relocation, and disruption of ties with children and community—all underlying the presenting problem of the suicidal wife and all related to a maladjustment to retirement. The process of therapy for the Berry family included reframing as a central therapeutic tool.

The Berry family also illustrates the reemergence, now centrally, of old issues and conflicts that were formerly peripheral to daily living. The new experience of long hours together without the structure of work to manage time and emotional distance requires a redistribution of tasks and activities. Wives may speak of feeling suffocated by their husbands' continued presence. A genogram can be useful for examining expectations for retirement, as a preliminary to the step of restructuring.

Newly retired adults may also face the care of their own elderly parents, or a recent retiree may need to nurse an ill spouse. These responsibilities complicate the process of retirement and add the risk of raising old conflicts. Caretaking of other family members when coupled with retirement is an example of a high-risk situation that indicates the need for family involvement in any treatment. The issue of long-term care in itself is addressed more fully in the next chapter.

As we have implied, retirement is a time of increased marital conflict and risk of divorce for many older couples. Wives' feelings of suffocation and decreased freedom counterbalance the husbands' resentment at their wives' attempts to regulate their use of time. Or a retired father who has previously been immersed in his work may now turn to the adult children, thus displacing much of his wife's intense involvement with them. Perhaps a wife refuses to stop clinging to the child instead of turning to the now more available husband. Couple or intergenerational family therapy is an appropriate resource to utilize.

These are some of the more common situations likely to come to a clinician's attention. A less obvious result of retirement is the effect upon the adult children. Witnessing the distress of a parent at retirement may be a central though covert component of the anxiety of adult children who themselves are at the developmental stage of beginning a career. On the other hand an adult child may precipitously enter marriage when the mother begins to withdraw from her overinvolved mother-child relationship and to move closer to her husband at his retirement. These examples are strong indicators of the need for intergenerational family sessions. Many of the direct interventions would be suitable for use in the early stages of these problems, but more long-term situations might require indirect interventions.

Designing rituals for the transition to retirement is a valuable tool for intervention with the retiree and the family. A ritual can serve as a rite of passage with positive yet realistic connotations. It can also help a family prepare for and rehearse the redistributed tasks and roles. Rituals allow human service providers an opportunity to practice their creativity in affirming ways. As with most rituals, it is important to ensure that all family members have a part, if not in the design of the ritual, at least in its performance.

For example, a clinician might guide a family in using an ecomap, first to identify how each family member spent time prior to the retirement, and then how time is distributed since the transition. Relationships, connections with activities in the home and in the community, and other factors of daily living are highlighted. If this information is difficult for the family to formulate, a typical scenario, perhaps a gathering at mealtime, is acted out to allow family members to experience the quality of various relationships. Perhaps the husband and the wife demonstrate a characteristic dinner conversation. Then, using the example of the meal or another time of family gathering, the practitioner helps the family prepare and rehearse a different version of the scene that allows the family to reach its goals for distribution of time and consequently of relationships. Each family member is given a role that moves the family toward the shared objective for life after retirement.

As we have indicated in our examination of retirement, couples and families are affected significantly by a family member's retirement. However, aging couples face other issues as well.

AGING COUPLES, MARITAL ISSUES, DIVORCE IN LATER YEARS

The characteristics of older couples have a direct impact on any portrait of the elderly. Statistics from the U.S. Bureau of the Census reveal that in 1987, 75.1% of the men and 39.8% of the women over the age of 65 were married and living with their spouse. Another 2.5% of the men and 1.6% of the women were married but the spouse was absent. In addition, 3.9% of the men and 4.5% of the women were divorced, 13.9% of the men and 48.7% of the women were widowed, and 4.6% of the men and 5.3% of the women had never married.

The level of functioning of aging couples also has familial and social relevance. In Chapter 1, in the discussion of life cyle stages, we mentioned that the later life stage of the nuclear family has as its task to maintain individual and/or couple functioning and interests in the face of changes in physiological and social roles. The context for an elder's adoption of the new roles, tasks, and options is the family as well as the larger community. The preceding discussion of retirement addresses one of the major changes in role and its effect upon the couple. However, there are other dimensions significant for older couples.

Contemporary Trends

The period of the empty nest has lengthened because of greater longevity, somewhat earlier marriage, and having fewer children. It is not unusual to learn of a marriage lasting 40 years. Marriages now are surviving the last child's leaving home, whereas in 1890 the last child married about 2 years after the death of a parent.

Butler and Lewis observe that in contemporary society:

> Most parents have completed childbearing by their later forties and early fifties, leaving them an average of 13 years alone together, or one third of their entire married life. . . . The older couple married for many years will find they have a different marriage in old age than they had in middle or early life. (1982, p. 159)

Each spouse has experienced life as an individual and also as a marital partner. The partners may have become more alike or more different. Patterns of dominance may shift; women may assume a more active and responsible role than before. Conflicts may have diminished over time as the spouses became more tolerant of one another, or intensifying conflicts and rigidity may have been the case. And whatever their history, aging couples will face issues surrounding care during illness, household management, and emotional gratification.

Caregiving for an Elderly Spouse

Increased longevity and the developments of modern medicine make caregiving for the elderly a feature of our society. Yet caregiving for an elderly spouse is an expectation that is usually not a conscious concern until misfortune arrives. Because most women live longer than men and marry men older than themselves, women are more likely to be the ones to take on the role of caregiver for a spouse. Men marry younger women and die earlier, and therefore are less apt to be widowed; they can count upon having a healthy spouse to nurse them.

A study of elderly wives who cared for their disabled husbands indicated that this responsibility not unexpectedly produced low morale among the wives. The ability to provide constant care and surveillance, however, depended significantly upon the wife's level of health. The caregiving included a degree of emotional and physical strain, an increase in social isolation, and a reduction in finances (Wilson, 1990). Long-term care can exacerbate any of the wife's feelings of bitterness and a sense of exploitation, a situation at risk of worsening should she deny her feelings and maintain a facade that her husband's care is no burden. Her husband likely would perceive her frustration and respond accordingly with his own feelings of hurt and anger. Couple intervention, probably involving the other family generations at some point, would be clearly indicated in order to provide each spouse with guidance and reassurance. For example, the clinician would reframe the wife's feelings of exploitation as understandable, while also indicating the need for respite care for her husband to lighten her burden. Steps to obtain the needed assistance would be presented as an act of loving care for her husband, as it would renew her strength for further attention to both their needs. A family session or two would be held to identify intergenerational patterns of giving and taking, and to access supplemental sources of assistance in the care of the father.

A more severe version of the above situation is the case of an elderly spouse serving as the sole caregiver for the aged mate. Family intervention may be necessary in order to assess not only what support is required but also what is available. The human service provider should assist the family members in the negotiation and reallocation of tasks as well as in the procurement of community support services. Any guilt about obtaining external assistance should be reframed as a misguided attempt to be loving and helpful. (The issue of long-term care will be addressed more fully in Chapter 6.)

Divorce

The marriages of most older couples end because of death rather than divorce. Grandchildren and children serve as a bond holding the couple together. And after long years of marriage most spouses have made adjustments to each other in ways that they experience as adequately supportive to render the unknown of divorce less appealing. With many other losses in their lives, the familiarity and predictability of their marriage is of special value. Older couples may grumble but they are often very dependent upon each other for intimacy, personal services, and mutual support. Divorce can be more easily risked if the partners are middle-aged or younger, when more options and resources are available to them: "Thus, in general, divorce occurs before old age, if it is to occur at all, and older people perceive threats to themselves emanating from outside the marital relationship as more significant than those from within" (Butler & Lewis, 1982, p. 160).

Divorce does occur in later years, however, and its increased evidence is a contemporary trend. Divorce will be the most difficult for the person cut off emotionally from the extended family. Because divorce can polarize family members, the divorce may create a cutoff within the family and with friends, leaving the divorcing member with less support at the very time it is most needed. Clearly the clinician should seek family involvement in the treatment of issues of divorce in later life. This step may entail confronting and resolving some long-term family patterns of alienation, with accompanying hurts and possible fears of aging and death. Re-storying can enable families with histories of losses to resolve hurts in a way that opens new possibilities for connections. A genogram can be useful for identifying cutoffs in family relationships and possibilities for new sources of support.

Higher divorce rates and lower birthrates bring about a population of older women with neither spouse nor available child, the two most important social supports for the elderly. Reaching out to others and dating may be stressful when a relationship of many years ends in divorce. Although they are more vulnerable to isolation, neglect, and institutionalization, many women replace marital relationships with friendships or contacts with siblings (Goldberg, Kantrow, Kremen, & Lauter, 1986). Even friends and relatives who provide support and companionship often are not as committed as children or spouses, however, and relatives may live at a distance. Thus single, childless elders are at a special disadvantage because social policies tend to assume families can take responsibility for aged relatives (Goldberg et al, 1986). Family therapists, versed in the importance of systems and networks, should heed the need of these women to build support systems and be aware of the high risk of tragedy if they do not.

Remarriage

Another contemporary trend for couples and a phenomenon of increased longevity is the late marriage, sometimes called a "retirement marriage." This is increasingly an option after divorce or widowhood, especially for men who have a larger pool of mates from which to choose. Aged singles seek to meet future mates in the same ways as their younger counterparts, through groups, clubs, classes, friends, and relatives.

Whether seeking friendship or romance, elderly newlyweds bring to this marriage their previous expectations and patterns of interaction. An older groom accustomed to a dominant marital role, marrying an elderly bride who had been in a previous democratic marriage, is probably not headed for wedded bliss. What can compound the difficulty is if a spouse begins to compare the new mate with the former one. Conflicts that stem from roles and interactional behavior patterns that have been learned and reinforced over many years are more difficult to resolve than conflicts in specific areas such as finances and sexuality (Peterson, 1973). Treatment for such issues should be conjoint. An intergenerational approach can be useful for examining the couple's expectations for marital roles. The clinician should also include the extended family in the treatment to address any resistance by family members to the new marriage and to elicit support where it is available.

A common problem for older remarried couples is the negotiation of financial support for family members and the writing of wills. A significant factor in family adjustment to their elder member's remarriage is the amount of cooperation that continues with the former spouse and the ability to permit joint family participation at the children's and grandchildren's rituals. Of course some families are happy that their elder member has found someone for support and assistance.

Cohabitation

Remarriage of elders may create financial problems, may cause upset among their children, and may provide legal constraints. These concerns have led to a rise in elderly couples living together without marriage despite the social stigma that this entails for this generation (Walsh, 1980, p. 203).

Elder family members need to have the right to choose whether to marry or not. Some adult children, however, attempt to control this aspect of their parents' lives. They may fear losing an inheritance, may resist accepting for their parent another partner who seems to be replacing their biological parent, or may fear losing intimate emotional support from the parent considering remarriage.

The need for legal advice in instances of cohabitation is well delineated by Hughston and Hughston (1989) and includes a useful guide for items to be considered at the onset of the relationship.

Spousal Impoverishment

When one member of a couple enters a nursing home, the spouse at home may quickly become impoverished. Public policies requiring reduction of financial resources as a prerequisite for receiving payment for nursing homes, coupled with the high cost of long-term care, have created a major area of concern for the elderly. Any family resistance to the financial drain from high medical bills for their elder parents places the family members at a most painful point of prioritizing who will be the beneficiary of family funds. Such stressful issues need to be discussed openly, a task the human services provider can and should facilitate.

Sexuality

Not only are the marital problems of older couples frequently related to discrepant rates of change, the fear of death, and the relationship to children, but also they may stem from sexual discord. Many older couples remain sexually active into their elderly years, although usually with reduced frequency. However, aging and illness may have a physical or emotional impact upon sexual behavior. Surgery such as a colostomy may inhibit sexual expression. Women may feel less sexually attractive after a mastectomy. Men with prostate conditions may experience reduced sexual drive. It is reported that men over the age of 60 have more organically based sexual dysfunction than women of the same age. For men the dysfunction is primarily impotence; for women, painful intercourse (Garrison, 1989).

Like younger people, the elderly respond with anxiety to threats of sexual impotence and lack of fulfillment. In addition, older adults must live in a world focused upon youth, the physical appearance of youth, and the sexual abilities of youth, and they must function within that social climate. Our culture prevails especially upon women to appear youthful in order to feel sexual or even generally desirable. An older-looking woman is expected to be asexual.

Elders may attempt to rationalize such concerns with a pretense of disinterest in sex. Of course a low level of sexual behavior may represent a lifetime pattern of attributing little importance to sexuality. A decline in sexuality in later years merits attention, however, and should not be attributed to aging. Instead the clinician should assess and treat any underlying issues of anger or hostility toward the spouse, perhaps stemming from issues of retirement or a change in physical functioning or a depression.

Normal in the aging process is a general slowing in the male response to sexual stimuli. The sexual response cycle from excitement to resolution proceeds at a slower pace. An older man uninformed of this change may be at high risk of developing secondary impotence if he becomes anxious when he cannot respond sexually to his partner at will or cannot reach orgasm as quickly as before. He and his partner need guidance and reassurance to enable them to enjoy this new developmental stage. The male, now better able to lengthen the period of foreplay and to experience less pressure to reach orgasm, can more easily control and coordinate his pleasure with that of his wife (Whitbourne, 1990). His male self-esteem need not suffer.

The older wife in turn faces her own issues. She is beyond menopause and no longer needs to consider birth control and pregnancy. She may experience a heightened sexual interest as a result. She may need help in overcoming the inhibitions of her generation that attribute sexual initiative solely to the male, now that her mate's sexual response is more placid. The human service provider may also need to assist the older woman with any feelings of shame or revulsion toward her aging body.

Alcohol and pressures from late-life careers can decrease significantly any elder's sexuality. (Substance abuse is addressed more fully in Chapter 6.)

Couple work is important to ferret out any attitudes and attendant cues from either partner that reinforce the other's negative self-image. Myths of aging as well as interference from extended families need to be addressed. Sexuality for those over 65 has too often been viewed as "immoral, inappropriate, and a foolish attempt to regain lost youth and vigor" (Whitbourne, 1990, p. 28). The "dirty old man" and the asexual grandma linger as destructive stereotypes.

Problems and Treatment of Aging Couples

We have referred to the central part played by families in contemporary issues that couples may face: those of retirement, long-term care of a spouse, divorce, remarriage, cohabitation, spousal impoverishment, and sexuality. These issues illustrate the crucial role of family treatment in assisting the couple with their problems. Not only do we advocate marital therapy when a spouse is in distress; we also emphasize the need to facilitate family involvement as much as possible, preferably in sessions including most if not all family members. If family members, including the couple, resist the integration of others into the treatment plan, the therapist should be wary of underlying myths of aging relegating the couple to the status of needing no help, wanting no help, or being beyond help. Family members holding significant power can be invited to planning sessions with later involvement for follow-up if they are unavailable for the preferred span of treatment. And telephone consultation may be an option. At the least, as was the case for the Berry family presented in Chapter 1, family members need to be kept informed of developments throughout the course of treatment.

Fortunately, many younger members enjoy the elder couple's well-earned opportunity to reestablish preparenthood patterns of relating to one another while reaping the rewards of the comfort and reassurance that come from many years together. The older couple serves as a rich model of aging for subsequent generations. However, some families may resist the independent functioning of their older members. This resistance may stem from a fear of death, their own as well as their elders'. Or adult children, especially women, who overly depend upon the caregiver role for self-definition, may attempt to avoid blame by overprotection of the elderly couple. Jealousy of the older couple is not uncommon in dysfunctional families. The general issue of resistance to elderly independence is addressed more fully in Chapter 6.

DEATH AND LOSSES

The major fears of older adults are fear of pain, indignity, loneliness and depersonalization during dying, and the possibility of dying alone. Few older adults have the opportunity to die at home as their parents and older relatives did. Over 50% of all deaths of older adults occur in hospitals, another 20% in nursing homes. The emphasis in these institutions is on physical care, not emotional concerns, although recent awareness of the need for support for the terminally ill has changed some of the rigid rules that limit visitors and intimate family contact. Hospice was designed to enable older adults to die in dignity, surrounded by their loved ones. It does not always work that way. Insurance and personal finances may serve to restrict access to such a program; families may deny the need for support because of their own unwillingness to address realities. Elders may worry about burdening survivors with the expenses of their dying.

Care of the dying includes physical care of the dying person, easing the pain and other discomforts, and giving emotional support. Through reminiscence and life review, with or without other aspects of therapy, the older adult is assisted in putting his or her affairs in order. Care entails facilitating the elderly dying at home when possible, because this is the preferred location for most people. Care also involves support for the dying person's family and loved ones who are at risk of increased somatic complaints, illness, and even death (Butler & Lewis, 1982).

Preparation for Death

Many can accept death with peace. It may even be welcomed as a relief from pain and anguish. One's view of impending death is closely related to the resolution of life's experiences and problems. A sense of having made a contribution to others may provide a satisfaction with the purpose of life. Deep religious beliefs and philosophical attitudes promote acceptance.

The process of facing death and working through the feelings begins at a different time for each person. For some the awareness that their remaining time to live is limited comes early, perhaps precipitated by the loss or near-death of a loved one. For others the signs of aging are the signal. Some deny until the very end. Resolution of feelings about death and coming to terms with their mortality may be responsible for what is perceived as the serenity and wisdom of some older adults.

The Process of Dying

Kubler-Ross (1969, 1975) developed a well-known model of five psychological stages of dying. It is now believed that these stages ranging from denial to acceptance occur in conflicting, overlapping, or alternating steps. These steps are influenced by factors such as age, gender, ethnicity and culture, personality, family history, and social setting. Understanding the various stages can be helpful in working with the dying and their families, as long as they are not adhered to rigidly without recognition of the elder's individuality.

In the first stage, that of denial, the person refuses to believe the evidence of impending death. The denial may be expressed indirectly, as in avoiding a medical examination or refusing to discuss the illness. The denial may be more overt as in flat statements that the person is well and experiencing only a minor medical inconvenience, or that the doctors do not know what they are talking about. Denial often is present as an avoidance of making arrangements appropriate to the illness. Whatever the form of denial, it is not the counselor's responsibility to confront the person with the reality at this stage. Nor is it appropriate to support with enthusiasm any unrealistic plans for the future. Argument and confrontation would likely be futile or could serve to solidify the denial. Being available as a gentle listener may be the best one can do to help the person through this period and on to the next.

The second stage is anger. The prospect of death cannot any longer be denied. The denial is replaced with anger and rage at the injustice and unfairness of life's ending. And it is not only the dying person who may be expressing anger, but also the family members and/or hospital staff. Relatives may be feeling helpless, thinking they did not do enough to keep the person well. Family members may also be angry because of the expected loss, of being abandoned and left alone. The dying elder may express anger at everyone and everything without any apparent justification. The task of the clinician is to hear and acknowledge the anger, not to stop it—to accept the anger without becoming angry too. The specifics of the anger need not make sense.

The third stage is that of bargaining. The person attempts to make a deal with God or fate in return for life. Forms of bargaining include embracing a regimen of exercise or diet and other means of remaining youthful. The family too may engage in bargaining, seeking magic potions or cures for their loved one, or even offering a sacrifice of time, activity, or personal growth. Bargaining implies some level of hope, which is easier for most people to manage than anger. A clinical understanding of this phenomenon is important. A support of unrealistic expectations, however, would contribute to an exaggeration of the usual letdown of entering the next stage.

Depression is the fourth stage. Bargaining no longer offers any hope. The dying person begins a preparatory grief over the loss of life and of loved ones. As long as there is life, there is opportunity for resolution and reinterpretation, but now the time to achieve goals and make major changes is limited. There is a reality to this depression. Depression is contagious, and family members may avoid a dying relative who is in a profound depression because of their own pain. Thus it is especially important that the clinician remain available to the dying. All that may be needed is to listen or to "be in silence" with the person. A quiet sharing of the therapist's own sense of depression about the elder's situation can be supportive. False encouragements are to be avoided; they could convey that the dying person is not understood, is truly alone.

The fifth and last stage is that of acceptance and a quiet anticipation of the impending death. This feeling of peace is not reached by everyone, but serves as the goal toward which efforts are directed. This stage includes a gradual detachment from the world, including family and loved ones. It is thus the hardest stage for the family to accept as they face being left to rebuild their lives without their relative. They may resist the elder's matter-of-fact attitude toward dying. Terminally ill elders feel frustrated and abandoned when well-meaning loved ones do not treat seriously their impending death. It is a time for the elder, and of course the family, to finish old business. Families and close friends should be helped to come say their last good-byes, to share what their lives together have meant and how the person will be missed. Eventually the elder may ask to see only family members and a few friends, then just the children, and finally only the spouse. In that case the clinician should help the family understand that this is a gradual separation that comes from having worked through the process of dying, that it is a healthy and normal detachment, not a rejection. At this stage the family may need the most support, the dying member the least.

For a more detailed presentation of the stages of dying and their management, the reader is referred to the writings of Kubler-Ross (1969, 1975) and Herr and Weakland (1979).

Helping the Family

When the dying elder is the primary client, the clinician is in a position more parallel to that of family members than in any other counseling situation (Herr & Weakland, 1979). Thus the suggestions for the counselor also apply to family members, although roles for the family are usually more difficult because of their greater involvement.

Family members should be encouraged to be gentle and compassionate with their loved one while also realistic about the approaching death. They should be informed of the danger of rejecting their elder by continual cheerfulness or unrealistic optimism. However, family understanding cannot be forced. Families will be experiencing their own stages of grief similar to those of their dying relative and may need extensive support and guidance through times of denial, anger, bargaining, depression, and finally acceptance. The therapist should be available to hear their concerns and to respond gently to their feelings. Family members may need to be encouraged to obtain some relief from the grieving process, going to a movie or seeking out a friend, or perhaps having a cup of tea or warm bath.

Tolerating the family's anger, like tolerating the anger of the dying family member, takes a certain amount of awareness, compassion, and patience. But it is necessary. Kubler-Ross states the need well (1969):

> If we tolerate their anger, whether it is directed at us, at the deceased, or at God, we are helping them take a great step towards acceptance without guilt. If we blame them for daring to ventilate such socially poorly tolerated thoughts, we are blameworthy for prolonging their grief, shame, and guilt which often results in physical and emotional ill health. (p. 180)

"Anticipatory grief" is another aspect of the process of dying. It is the withdrawal from the dying person, who then is grieved as though already dead. The time has not yet come for the final separation from the dying relative, yet the family member cannot tolerate the waiting. Thus, in this situation, the older person who may have resolved the difficult feelings about death faces it alone without the needed human comfort and support. Hospital regulations with their short and limited visiting hours and lack of accommodations for intimate family interactions tend to promote anticipatory grief. An equally harmful alternative to anticipatory grief is a family member's clinging desperately to the dying person's presence. Or family members may displace their concern onto another family member. In such instances families need assistance with their feelings of helplessness and their inability to communicate effectively with the dying relative and each other.

It is often the dying family member who can be helpful to others in accepting the approaching death. Through sharing thoughts and feelings, beliefs and fears, the member near death can both model and facilitate communication with others. The peace and acceptance of a dying person who has worked through feelings about death can be of great support to family members. Through open sharing, family members can be relieved of their self-reproach and guilt for "not having done enough." It is essential that the clinician realize and accept the value of this process in order to facilitate family members' own grieving. Unfortunately practitioners, from their own anxieties and uncertainties, at times have engaged unwittingly in a competition with the dying person for the role of expert on the situation.

Families should be encouraged to maintain as much of their previous levels of activity as possible, to strike a balance between serving the dying member and serving their own needs. The entire household should not be totally disrupted. It is a commonly accepted principle that the spouse or near relatives of a dying person should continue connections with people and other activities, both as a support during the stress of the relative's dying process and as a facilitative step toward effective mourning after the death. It is cruel to expect one person to be the sole attendant, even though that may be the person's wish:

> Just as the terminally ill patient cannot face death all the time, the family member cannot and should not exclude all other interactions for the sake of being with the patient exclusively. He too has a need to deny or avoid the sad realities at times in order to face them better when his presence is really needed. (Kubler-Ross, 1969, p. 158)

At the time of near death, family members may be in conflict about whether to remain with their dying relative or to return home to tend to other aspects of their lives. Clinicians should understand this dilemma and consider the option of helping the family select a member who is most comfortable with death and therefore will stay with the dying person. The others can then feel less guilt or shame about avoiding this difficult time, knowing that their loved one will not die alone. The member present can be strengthened through witnessing the death if it is peaceful, but likely will need support for anguish if it is a painful death.

Families facing the death of one of their members will be at risk of developing emotional and/or physical symptoms if they are unable to address directly with each other the reality of the impending death:

> No matter how well-differentiated the family, the ability to remain open, to express one's thoughts and feelings and to remain nonreactive to the other's anxiety, is related to the intensity and duration of the stress. The longer and more intense the family stress, the more difficult it is for family relationships to remain open and the more likely it is that dysfunction will develop. (Carter & McGoldrick, 1980, p. 233)

Death and Mourning

> No one ever told me that grief felt so like fear. I am not afraid, but the sensation is like being afraid. The same fluttering in the stomach, the same restlessness, the yawning. I keep on swallowing.
>   At other times it feels like being mildly drunk, or concussed. There is a sort of invisible blanket between the world and me. I find it hard to take in what anyone says. Or perhaps, hard to want to take it in. It is so uninteresting. Yet I want the others to be about me. I dread the moments when the house is empty. If only they would talk to one another and not to me.

Thus C. S. Lewis (1961, p. 7) vividly describes the experience of grief in mourning. Grief refers to the complex painful feelings and the emotional response to loss; mourning is the process that one lives through during bereavement and includes various rituals; bereavement is the state of having experienced the loss of a loved one (Williams, 1989, p. 226). A person will mourn in a "journey of healing" that usually lasts 18 months to 4 years. The mourning and grief vary in relation to the survivor's attachment to the loved one as well as to the mourner's personality, culture, past experiences of loss, and support system.

Patterns of Mourning

Williams (1989) lists four tasks for the accomplishment of mourning. Not all family members finish all tasks, thus extending bereavement. The tasks are to experience the pain of grief, to find and utilize a support system for assistance in grieving and for adjustment to the environment, to handle the practical matters resulting from the death, and to accept the reality of the loss and to say good-bye.

Bereavement may begin with a few days of initial shock. This period is followed by a time of intense mourning. It may entail problems eating and sleeping, physical symptoms that mimic those of the dead loved one, even almost hallucinatory experiences of the presence of the deceased in voice or in person. Finally, a gradual lessening of grief and a reawakening to life occur. Grief is a necessary and painful part of healing that is unpredictable and individual. The role of family members is central to the course of successful mourning; social support has been shown to be a reliable predictor of successful adjustment. Therefore family therapy is indicated for any presenting problems related to suspected incomplete mourning. Family members should be assessed for unresolved losses of their own that may interfere with their assistance to the mourning relative. Mourning rituals can be useful for resolution of issues from a previous death. Sometimes all that is needed is the permission to reminisce about former loved ones and talk about how those feelings have been triggered by the current bereavement. Or a visit to the grave site may be healing despite the pain involved in doing so.

Grief that goes awry falls into several common patterns (Williams, 1989). Grief becomes prolonged and excessive and thus chronic, without satisfactory completion. Or grief is delayed because of inhibited, suppressed, or postponed responses. Grief may be exaggerated because the grief-related anxiety is magnified and becomes a phobia, or because the feelings of hopelessness develop into despair. Or grief becomes masked or repressed, leading to physical symptoms or maladaptive behavior.

Most physical and emotional symptoms disappear with time, although depression often lasts several months. Family members with preexisting illnesses are at greater risk of problems during bereavement.

Abnormal mourning has been correlated with precipitating a new illness. Widowed men up to the age of 75 are more likely to die than married men of the same age (Williams, 1989).

Family Responses to Bereavement

Bereavement affects the family system in many ways. The degree of disruption to the family system is related to several factors (Herz, 1980). The more significant variables are the timing of the death in the family life cycle, the nature of the death or preceding illness, the openness of the family system, and the family position of the deceased member.

In general, the farther along the elder is in the life cycle, the less the family will experience stress from the elder's death. A family member who dies in old age is perceived as having achieved life's tasks, but death or serious illness at an earlier age is considered to indicate an incomplete life and is apt to be more disruptive to the family (Herz, 1980). It is clear that family stress is strongly related to the nature of any illness preceding the death and the degree of whatever debilitation was involved. Stress also arises from family members' awareness that the death of the older generation brings them closer to their own deaths.

Family members should be open with each other about the death and their related feelings. Otherwise they are at risk of developing emotional or physical symptoms. The ability to express one's thoughts and feelings and to respond to others without reaction to anxiety is difficult in the best of families. The longer and more intense the family stress, the more difficult it is for the family to communicate openly. In addition unresolved previous losses may have produced dysfunctional patterns of grieving and support that indicate the need for family intervention. The essence of families with a dying member is one of isolation that excludes external networks. Moreover, after the funeral the social gap may be felt the most, when friends no longer come to visit and bring food and the frequency of telephone calls declines. Effective resolution of these aspects of grieving may require family counseling to build the needed support. Ecograms and genograms are helpful for assessing family patterns of response to loss and availability of internal and external resources. Family members may reminisce in a healing fashion about earlier years of better times or about losses, when given the encouragement to do so. Rituals may be designed to complete unfinished mourning and thus to open the way to access new or renewed means of interaction with others.

The loss of a spouse brings special needs. Social relationships are altered and the surviving spouse may feel unwelcome in couple-oriented activities, often a response based upon reality. An overly dependent wife may have difficulty assuming more responsibility for her needs. Mourning a long-term relationship that was conflictual usually is more complex. No matter what the composition of the marriage, the surviving spouse faces practical matters such as where to live, how to manage financial matters, how to spend time. These decisions should be delayed if possible until some degree of mourning has been accomplished. Grieving is not complete until the surviving spouse has been through at least one year of anniversaries: birthdays, wedding anniversary, anniversary of the spouse's death, Christmas or other religious occasions, Thanksgiving, and other holidays. Creating new rituals for these milestones is part of the healing process.

Not all deaths have equal importance in a family. The more significant the deceased member, the more likely it is that an emotional shock wave will run through the family system. This ripple effect comes from the disrupted equilibrium in the family system as well as from the family's tendency to deny its dependency when that dependency is great (Herz, 1980). The roles of a deceased, central family member must be reassigned, a situation conducive to highlighting any competition between members. And if the dead elder was emotionally overly responsible, the correspondingly less responsible members likely will face a difficult adjustment. In family sessions a focus on the strengths of the deceased member can lead the way to unleashing energy for the discussion of who else has strengths and abilities that can be recruited in the redistribution of roles and responsibilities.

Families may need assistance with their children's mourning. Children's needs may be forgotten at the time of a family member's death. If family members do not have the energy to respond appropriately, they can be encouraged to enlist a familiar neighbor or less involved relative for helping the children ask their questions or express their fears. Children react differently to a family member's death. The child's age, the closeness to the deceased member, the family rules and prohibitions about expressing feelings, are all relevant factors. Counselors should be well informed about the meaning of death for different ages of development.

Mourning Rituals

Butler and Lewis (1982) speak of the importance of mourning rituals:

> Learning how to mourn productively and restoratively requires models in ritual and custom as well as in personal experiences with others who mourn. Lack of such support can prolong depression and leave grief unresolved. (p. 78)

Unfortunately our culture views death as a taboo, leaves much of the arrangements and thus the control to the funeral director, and attributes emotional behavior to being weak. Exaggerated depression, aimless busyness, deification of the deceased, cold denial of others' grief as well as one's own—these are possible outcomes of societal repression. This framework makes it especially difficult for family members to behave differently and to be more supportive of one another.

Many rituals in modern life have been eliminated. Included are the custom of wearing black clothing or arm bands or of withdrawing from social events for a period of time. Or rituals that are religious or involve the support of friends are practiced only in part. Their more modern replacements, such as numbing the feelings with tranquilizers or receiving consolation from funeral directors instead of family members or friends, are questionable in their effectiveness.

Funerals can be useful in offering an opportunity to say good-bye to the deceased in the company of supportive friends. The preparations for the funeral, and the event itself, are ways of crystallizing the reorganization of the family now that one member has died. The funeral is a rite of passage that marks a new developmental stage in the family life cycle. Funerals provide several opportunities for changes in the family system (Friedman, 1980). Family members can shift or take on responsibilities. Contact with distant or estranged relatives and friends can be reestablished. Information about the family history can be affirmed or obtained. Funerals are a forum for coming face to face with the primal forces of life and one's own mortality. Triangles of family relationships tend to surface at funerals and can be altered in the direction of more direct communication. And funeral rituals are an opportunity to reduce the debilitating effects of grief.

Rituals such as funerals are useful as therapeutic interventions. Family practitioners often help families design a funeral ritual for a long-deceased member when mourning remains unresolved. This intervention is presented in more detail in the next section.

Treatment Issues

The major purpose of family interventions in situations of death or terminal illness is the prevention of family symptomology and dysfunction during the illness and after the death (Herz, 1980). The family should be helped to manage the stress with the least intrusive interventions. Because the therapist is helpless to change the facts of the terminal illness or death, the locus for intervention is the family's emotional and communication systems.

Factual and direct terminology, with words such as *dead* or *dying* instead of *passing on* or *passed away*, helps maintain the reality. Forthright language indicates that the therapist is relatively comfortable with a discussion of death.

Establishing at least one open relationship between family members can unlock the family communication. The therapist might begin by seeking out the family member who looks the most uncomfortable and therefore may be willing to shift roles. A discussion between the therapist and one family member is to be avoided, however, as it may reduce the family's anxiety enough to inactivate any force toward change, and may even insert the therapist into a family triangle. Members should be encouraged to respect each others' different feelings and pace of mourning. A review of the lost relationship, with its positive and painful aspects, is part of the therapeutic discussion. The clinician should be alert to any issue of unresolved mourning from previous losses that prevents current healing.

It is important that the therapist remain calm and not react while being gently supportive: the practitioner may choose to share personal feelings with the dying elder and the family, but those actions should not be guided by emotions. This requires that the clinician has addressed and resolved most personal issues relating to death. Only then can an appropriate perspective be maintained by the human service provider.

The family may present secondary issues to distract themselves and the therapist from the trauma at hand. A few minutes may be devoted to the offered crises, but the major situation of the death must be kept in mind and closely monitored. A family genogram designed to indicate previous significant deaths and their management by the extended family can identify relevant patterns of mourning. The use of rituals should be part of such an assessment. In addition the genogram can reveal emotional responses to death and dying, whether it be angry confrontations about money, cutoffs, or depression.

Rituals are useful as therapeutic interventions. Family therapists often help families design a funeral ritual to expedite the process of mourning. Following are some guidelines for coaching families in creating such a ritual: It should be in keeping with the family's religious and philosophical beliefs. It should be as personalized as possible with the family members' input into its formation. And it should include discussion of the deceased member. There should be an opportunity to say good-bye. These guidelines are also appropriate for assisting the family when they are making choices about the loved one's funeral at the time of death.

The special needs of minority families should be part of the repertoire of any counselor addressing issues of bereavement. Helping a family manage a loss should include a respect for the family's culture and ethnicity. The family members' cultural values and timing regarding death and mourning are to be honored even though it is usually preferable to help families openly express their feelings about the death of their loved one. For example, in Irish families the discussion of death is apt to be considered morbid or crazy, and unresolved mourning may best be done in individual or conjoint sessions rather than with the total family present. For both African-American and Irish families, attendance at a well-planned funeral is important and a token of respect for the deceased; unlike the Irish, African-Americans would find a festive atmosphere at the funeral to be unacceptable. The Chinese feel great shame and a taboo against discussing a violent or untimely death. As McGoldrick and colleagues point out,

> It is extremely important that as therapists we become sensitive to the variety of meanings death can have for families from different cultural backgrounds. Even though these meanings are ever changing, the traditional cultural beliefs our clients hold about death will influence their ability to mourn and then move on. And, as therapists, our own beliefs will necessarily influence our ability to help our clients make sense of life's hardest problem: Death. (1986, p. 36)

Therapists are encouraged to explore their own experiences of losses and death. Unresolved grief issues can easily interfere with the ability to make meaningful and appropriate interventions. The offering of compassion and the maintenance of a clear perspective require a supportive objectivity that is diametrically opposed to readily triggered defensive reactions. The clinician should be open to the subjects of dying, death, and grief and be able to assess the individual features of the dying elder and the family:

> Work with the families of the dying, as with the dying themselves, is not a matter of simple interventions to make bad situations good. Yet as a counselor you can still help people avoid making a painful and difficult situation even worse, and at least sometimes to reach acceptance of the difficult realities together. These goals, while limited, are still worth your best efforts. (Herr & Weakland, 1979, p. 296)

SPIRITUALITY

Spirituality and the elderly—this is a topic rarely addressed in the literature. Spirituality is not measurable, and scientific studies are focused elsewhere. Traditional mental health teaches that spirituality or religion is suspect, perhaps unhealthy, and the role of the mental health worker very likely is to dispel such "illusions." In interviews with the clergy and mental health workers, it was easy to elicit vignettes about the elderly and their self-esteem or perhaps their reminiscences, but the conversation kept straying away from the topic of spirituality per se. This occurred despite the commonly held view that people turn increasingly to religion and spirituality as they age and approach death.

Alcoholics Anonymous in its various forms does a better job of addressing spirituality than do mental health professionals. Even in AA, however, the needs of spirituality in the context of aging are rarely the focus of a group.

Because spirituality itself is not often the focus of studies of the elderly and aging, it is even more unlikely that attention will be devoted to the role of the family in sustaining or promoting such spirituality. Although spirituality is a personal matter, it can be greatly enhanced if shared with others. Family members can be the first in line to be the benefactors and beneficiaries in that sharing.

Spirituality Defined

So what do we mean by spirituality? It is not synonymous with religion, which is a more circumscribed concept. Religion refers to an organized set of beliefs and the practices associated with the beliefs. When we speak of religion, being connected to a specific church or congregation comes to mind, although such membership is not a requisite for religion.

Spirituality and religion overlap somewhat, but spirituality is less concrete. By spirituality we refer to: "the transcendental relationship between the person and a Higher Being, a quality that goes beyond a specific religious affiliation, that strives for reverence, awe, and inspiration, and that gives answers about the infinite" (Peterson & Nelson, 1987, p. 35). A person's belief and understanding of the higher being, or higher power, is individualistic. One person may refer to that source of strength as God; another may hold a view of some less-defined, existential power of life.

Whatever the specifics of the definition, spirituality provides a sense of the meaning and purpose of life, a means of forgiveness, and a source of love and relatedness. Spiritual well-being, as formulated at the 1971 White House Conference on Aging, is "the affirmation of life in a relationship with a God, self, community, and environment that nurtures and celebrates wholeness" (Blazer, 1991, p. 62). The conference identified dimensions of spiritual need that warrant attention. They include socio-cultural sources of spiritual needs. Spirituality can also provide relief from anxieties and fears. In addition spirituality should serve as a foundation for the preparation for death, for personality integration, for personal dignity, and a philosophy of life. When these spiritual needs are fulfilled, spiritual well-being follows.

The Importance of Spiritual Factors in Treatment

Before discussing the treatment of issues related to spirituality, we wish to emphasize the necessity of assessing what role a spiritual life plays for the older adult and family members. It seems strange that the overreaching and compelling needs mentioned above do not often attract the spotlight of therapy. Assessment of the spiritual component of a client should be a routine matter. It is essential for understanding the person and developing a treatment plan.

Because spirituality is not readily measured or observed, it is not a simple task to obtain such information. In addition, religion and spirituality tend to become more private for very old adults as they turn inward at the end of life. Moreover members of the current generation of older adults often were raised not to talk about such subjects to begin with, and they view them as too personal to be put into words.

A helpful way to begin therapy is for the worker to pose commonplace questions such as what the person's religious affiliation is. Does the elder attend a place of worship? What were the family practices when the older person was a child? What are the family practices now? The family and its rituals, beliefs, and customs are crucial aspects of any assessment of spirituality. The likeliness of an elder being involved with a religious congregation as a place for sharing spiritually within a community is related to the family pattern of spiritual practices. When elders are involved with a religious group, often one finds that this has been a lifetime pattern that began with the family of origin, although there may have been periods of less active involvement. The role of spirituality in one's life is strongly influenced by the family, both the ancestors and the current significant members.

An understanding of an older adult's spirituality should include the elder's specific practices as well as those of other family members. How supportive or detrimental are they for handling the losses of aging and the incumbent stress? Are they conducive to the spiritual integrity and dignity of the elder? Do they provide a support network for the older adult within the family, within the community?

Assessment should then address the meaning of life. Why does the person go on living? What is the elder's source of meaning and purpose in life? For some it will be their faith and spiritual beliefs; for some it will be something specific such as the visit of a special family member or friend; for some life may have no meaning. Elders who return in later years to activity in a religious community often do so primarily to pose questions about the meaning of life and death, with a decrease in social isolation being an important but a secondary motive. When in an environment of respect and openness, elders usually exhibit their interest in continuing to grow, both spiritually and emotionally. They pose intense spiritual questions. Although they are aware of the limited time remaining to live and that each day may have a precious quality to it, healthy older adults usually do not live with a sense of impending death. Instead life becomes more open to them as they are freed of distractions.

One needs to ask whether guilt or forgiveness are significant factors in the elder's life. A heightened sensitivity to criticism or a tendency to blame others for one's own faults may mask an inability to accept and forgive oneself. Family members may have a significant impact upon this situation as their own issues of guilt or insecurity come into play. Reminiscence or life review, alone or preferably in the company of supportive friends or family members, can alleviate inordinate guilt and remove barriers to a fuller experience of spiritual well-being. Re-storying is another appropriate intervention in such a situation.

We have mentioned that older adults may be hesitant or reluctant to verbalize their spiritual needs or concerns. One hospice worker in nursing homes has found that poetry is a medium that is less threatening to many older adults. Writing a journal or participating in writing support groups can facilitate the expression of thoughts and feelings regarding spirituality. This expression is not only healthful, it is also useful for an assessment of spirituality.

Treatment

First of all, human service providers should become aware of the prevalent need of older adults to address issues of spirituality. This need often increases as the person approaches death. Spiritual concerns should not be lost in a diagnosis of depression. There are unfortunate instances of psychiatric staff missing the client's underlying questions about the meaning of life, with the client withdrawing from service after what might have been a courageous effort to seek help in the first place. Human service providers who are uncomfortable addressing spiritual issues should, at the very least, have available a referral network of those who make this realm their specialty. Perhaps most important of all, clinicians should make the effort to reflect upon their own attitudes about spirituality, to determine to what extent they may be ignoring or even repressing the spiritual aspect of their clients' presenting problems and needs. For those human service providers who wish to learn more about spirituality and aging, a prime resource is the elders themselves. Encouraging them to talk about themselves can provide profound spiritual insights into the process of aging.

One of the pleasures of aging seems to be a relaxation of defenses, a discarding of illusions, compelling necessities, and controlling addictions, which frees older adults to seek new tasks to take on. Yet elders are also often lonely. If no family is available, they may be forced to live with other older adults and interact primarily with other elders because our society does not lend itself readily to forming surrogate families. Because of their loneliness and available energy, elders often find the role of advocacy a fulfilling one. This activity usually is on behalf of the elderly, but need not be limited to a particular age group. Advocacy, especially if in a communal setting such as a religious congregation, provides an opportunity for the older adult to be lively and therefore less at risk of the pain of loneliness. Clergy are aware that, when the religious lives of active elders occur in a communal setting where the interactions are with all age groups, those lives are less likely to be fearful. Families may look askance at advocacy and other new directions as being a sign of senility or futility; they need assistance in understanding and supporting this channeling of energies.

Families may interfere with elders' resolution of spiritual issues. This may be because of family members' uncertainty about their own religious or spiritual beliefs, their discomfort with an elder's spiritual beliefs and practices, or their unwillingness to address their own mortality. A clinically skilled member of the clergy of the family's religion can be a valuable ally in a family session, providing comfort to family members and support for their individual differences of belief while dispelling erroneous concepts of religious teachings, which so often underlie painful worries.

Family members who are facing separation through death of their elder loved member may resist acknowledging any differences between them. It is as if the impending loss through death is so painful that any difference of spirituality that relates to death is too much to bear.

Issues of religion or spirituality may also serve as a disguise for other difficulties. An example is the Thomas family in which role expectations were quite rigid and long-standing conflict was played out in the form of religious and spiritual activities and concerns. Mr. Thomas was a military man; activity in the church was central in his life and culminated in his election to a lay position in the parish. Mrs. Thomas had participated in social activities at the church throughout her marriage and after her husband's death, but the family's description of her was "not a religious person." Their two sons had built their lives around church activity, one becoming a church pastor, the other a military man who was an active church member. When their mother was dying, the family conflicts were exacerbated. The military son was greatly upset about his mother's calm acceptance of the parish pastor's not coming to give her the last rites. He would not entertain his brother's supportive opinions and persisted in his fear that his mother would "go to hell." This fear heightened when the minister at the funeral praised his mother without casting any doubts upon the quality of her afterlife. The rift between the two sons, which reflected a less overt and intense degree of the rift between the parents, escalated almost to the point of physical violence as the last parent's life was nearing a close. This rift was cloaked in terms of concerns about spirituality and religion that served to disguise the other problems. The true spiritual issues in the family could not be resolved until after the mother's death. Then skilled human service providers facilitated some reconciliation of the brothers by addressing the subjects of hierarchy, boundary, and family role expectations. It is not known what spiritual issues remained unresolved for Mrs. Thomas at her death. True to her lifetime pattern of holding such matters private, she gave no sign of having discussed her beliefs or fears with anyone, certainly not with her sons.

SUMMARY

Spiritual growth is a developmental process and thus parallels the course of the life cycle. This chapter has addressed aspects of a person's later years in that cycle and family involvement in that process, with suggestions for treatment when management of the process goes awry. We now proceed to explore issues that are not necessarily associated with the life cycle, but that all too often impact older adults and their families.

Chapter 6

FAMILY TREATMENT FOR DIFFICULTIES ENCOUNTERED BY THE ELDERLY

This chapter presents various issues that older adults and their families may face. The issues are not considered to be part of the normal process of aging but unfortunately are prevalent in our culture. They vary in the amount of attention ordinarily paid to them: from long-term care, which is a topic familiar in everyday conversation; to depression, which is often expected to be part of "normal" aging; to elder abuse, which is glossed over most of the time. We begin with an issue that many families find anxiety-producing or embarrassing to discuss, that of the independence of their older member.

FAMILY RESISTANCE TO ELDERS' INDEPENDENCE

Families may be intrusive or they may be enmeshed. The primary goal of their treatment may well be the liberation of elder members. Hartman and Laird (1983) give the following assessment of the parameters of that process:

AUTHORS' NOTE: The section on substance abuse was written in collaboration with Paul Estenson, Ph.D., affiliate at the Ann Arbor Center for the Family, Ann Arbor, Michigan, and consulting psychologist to the Older Adult Chemical Dependency Program and Older Adult Recovery Center, Chelsea Community Hospital, Chelsea, Michigan.

For most older people and their families, transition to old age, with all of the accommodations and adaptation required, is accomplished without professional help. Family networks remain intact, younger family members offer appropriate help and support as needed, medical problems may emerge but are often manageable and not catastrophic, extrafamilial human and economic resources are sufficiently available, and needed progressive care is available through familial and social arrangements.

For those coming to the attention of social workers, however, these transitions are not being smoothly accomplished. The professional's challenge is to help the aging person and family to resolve problems generated by illness, increasing need for care, social and economic isolation, and lack of appropriate resources. . . .

An understanding of the dynamics of family systems and of aging can help a worker deal with the complex and often highly intense transactional sequences initiated in such situations. Families become more fused and more caught up in reactive patterns when faced with stress. Dependence is intimately connected with fusion. It is difficult to take an "I-position" when one is realistically dependent for survival on the very person or system from which one is attempting to differentiate; it is probably to this issue some refer when they liken the conditions of aging to those of childhood. (p. 365)

The myth that the process of aging involves a role reversal of parent and child contradicts the reality that a parent remains the parent and never becomes the child, no matter how frail or impaired the elder may be. This myth can easily contribute to intergenerational conflict and a distortion of roles.

Issues of dependence, independence, and the reality of interdependence are central to the aging process. Older adults maintaining that they need no one and nothing from others may be extending a life pattern of "independence"; yet the price they pay is loneliness. They forgo much of the connectedness to others that for most people is a support and foundation for late life adjustment. Moreover pure isolation and total independence are illusions, as we all are interdependent, like it or not. Families dealing successfully with issues of "independence" accept the reality of interdependence. Conversely those successful in addressing loneliness are aware that interdependence includes some degree of loneliness.

When loneliness of an elder member is the presenting problem, feelings of low self-worth and issues of control are to be suspected. The older adult may be concerned about being worthwhile when unable to be totally self-sufficient and may be fearful of daring to be influenced by others (Herr & Weakland, 1979). Family members may urge a counselor to "motivate" their older parent, a demand masking a wish to manipulate the elder in the battle for control. In some instances, adult children leading frenzied lives as an avoidance of a pressing demand label their elders' more peaceful pace as loneliness, and their own resentment as worry. Clinical efforts to suggest activities and alternatives, in attempts at first-order change, would be unfruitful if concerns such as the above were not addressed. Circular questioning in a family session can be helpful for illuminating the function of the elder's "loneliness" and the degree of struggle over control. What comes to light may be a difference in the family members' definitions of loneliness, and then loneliness becomes reframed as a difference of opinion.

In power struggles, as one participant pushes harder for change, the other participant holds equally steadfast to resist change. At the level of the family, this struggle may be manifested in the way care is given elder members. Loss of functioning may result from overprotection and unneeded coddling. This produces a situation that indicates the need for human service providers to coach the family in alternative behavioral responses while being wary of collusion with the family's attitude that the elder is not capable.

Patterns of care may hide other problems such as marital conflict among the adult children, resulting in resistance to elder members' attempts at autonomy. This creates a chronic situation in which the elder's problem or dependence is a solution to another problem in the family system. Such dilemmas usually require an intervention at the level of second-order change in order to move the combatants off dead center and to release the elder members from being infantilized or unduly restrained.

Some practical guidelines for adult children talking constructively with their parents include the following (Kutner, 1990): First of all, goals should be realistic; children should accept the reality that the parents will not be ready to make major changes; that if they have been arguing for years, they will continue to regulate their lives in that or similar ways. Second, the parents should be approached by the adult children as a group, not singly, especially if the parents' health or safety is of concern. Third, adult children should avoid taking sides in a parental conflict, yet need to listen to each parent. After one parent presents an opinion, an adult child should solicit the other parent's view of the matter at hand. Fourth, adult children, even if clinicians by profession, should remember that they cannot be their parents' therapists. Listening and providing support and giving advice should be devoid of attempts to solve the parents' problems or to manage their lives.

The lengthening of the life span in recent times has created a period of life that has few role models from the past. Maggie Kuhn, the co-founder of the Grey Panthers and a champion of the elderly, has provided such a role model for later life. She conceptualizes the process of aging as one that involves a pride in age, in one's history and experience, in one's ability to change and to be innovative. She espouses the combination of the wisdom and experience of the elderly with the new knowledge and energy of the young as a source of future direction for our society. Her pride in her "well-earned wrinkles" is a banner for us all as we and our family members enter the later years.

LONG-TERM CARE

The lengthening of the life span brings the potential not only to have wrinkles, but also to experience poor health. Illness is a prominent concern for older adults. Although most elderly maintain adequate good health, they fear the loss of physical or mental well-being by becoming ill with a chronic, painful malady or by being inflicted with a progressively deteriorating illness.

A Classification of Illness

Rolland (1987) presents a comprehensive categorization that is useful in understanding the impact of chronic illness upon the affected individual and the family.

Onset of Illness

Illnesses at onset are defined as acute (such as strokes) or gradual (such as Parkinson's disease). Both types may necessitate the same amount of adaptation, but adaptation to an acute-onset illness must occur in a shorter period of time. Thus families with an ability to mobilize crisis management skills quickly will be better able to manage acute-onset types of illnesses. Those skills consist of the capability to endure high levels of emotion, to shift clearly defined roles with flexibility, to problem solve, and to obtain external resources.

Course of Illness

Chronic illnesses can also be characterized by the course the illness takes. The course can be progressive (as in Alzheimer's disease or emphysema), constant (as in spinal cord injury or a single stroke), or relapsing/episodic (as in hypertension, shingles, or gout). Progressive-course illnesses allow emotional preparation with time to locate appropriate resources. The unremitting demand for adaptation and role change, however, permits little relief. Caregivers experience increasing strain from the continual addition of new tasks and from exhaustion.

Constant-course illnesses are characterized by an initial episode followed by a stabilized, permanent degree of impairment. Although the family faces exhaustion over time, there are no demands for new roles after the initial adjustments have been made.

Relapsing or episodic illnesses are those that alternate periods of few or no symptoms with periods of recurrence of symptoms. The crises and remissions are unpredictable in terms of time of onset and duration. Families managing this sort of illness must alternate between two forms of organization and are at risk of stress from the frequent transitions between crisis and normalcy.

Outcome of Illness

The third category of chronic illnesses as conceptualized by Rolland is by outcome. A continuum of outcomes of chronic illnesses extends from no typical threat of shortening the life span (such as arthritis) to a fatal outcome (such as AIDS or metastatic cancer). Illnesses intermediate to these extremes are apt to be less clear in outcome and include those that shorten the life span (such as cardiovascular disease) and those that threaten sudden death (such as hemophilia). What outcome is expected will determine the family's opportunity for anticipatory grief. Moreover when the possibility of loss is unclear and the illness may result in shortened life or sudden death, families are at risk of becoming overprotective with secondary gains for the ill member.

Incapacitation

The extent, kind, and timing of incapacitation interact with the three categories of onset, course of illness, and outcome. This complexity of features has a major impact upon the family. Impairment can be cognitive (as in Alzheimer's disease), of the senses (as in blindness or deafness), motor (as in paralysis from a stroke), related to energy production (as in cardiovascular disease), disfiguring (as in cancer or advanced arthritis), or stigmatizing (as in AIDS). Incapacitation can be mild or intermittent, or it can occur only initially. For example, the incapacitation from a stroke is often the worst at onset and places demands upon the family for immediate adaptability. In addition the combined cognitive and motor incapacitation requires significant reassignment of roles. On the other hand incapacitation can be a more pervasive threat in cases such as Alzheimer's disease, but the progressive quality of that disease allows anticipatory planning by the family in cooperation with its ill member. Alcoholism is an example of a progressive disease, of gradual onset, that is incapacitating—an illness addressed more fully later in this chapter.

Phases of Illness

Chronic illnesses can be also classified in terms of time, that is, as composed of crisis, chronic, and terminal phases. The crisis phase consists of the symptomatic period preceding diagnosis, plus the beginning adjustment period during the initial treatment of the disease. Tasks for the family at this time include the following (Rolland, 1987):

Create a meaning for the illness event that maximizes a preservation of a sense of mastery and competency.

Grieve for the loss of the pre-illness family identity.

Move toward a position of acceptance of permanent change while maintaining a sense of continuity between its past and future.

Pull together to undergo short-term crisis reorganization.

In the face of uncertainty, develop a system of flexibility toward future goals. (p. 207)

The next phase, the chronic period, follows the initial diagnosis and readjustment and precedes the phase when issues of death have become central. The chronic phase can be of any length of time and is characterized by the day-to-day living with the specific features of the chronic illness. The task of the family at this period is to maintain normal functioning while managing the less-than-normal illness with its incumbent uncertainties. A goal is for all family members to obtain maximal autonomy despite the need for mutual dependency and care-giving. If the illness is fatal, this is a time of waiting, of "being in limbo."

Conversely if the illness is long-term and not immediately fatal, family exhaustion may ensue with relief coming only after the ill member's death.

The terminal phase was discussed in the previous chapter in the section addressing death and other losses. Briefly, the terminal phase begins when death is deemed inevitable. Tasks are those of separation and grief and the resolution of loss as the family assumes a life that incorporates the loss.

Life Cycle Stage

The life cycle stage of the family interacts with the timing of the family member's illness. A crisis of an older adult is a force toward family cohesion. If the family is at a point in the cycle that entails members moving outward, such as when adult children seek community involvement after their own children have been raised, then the illness of an aging parent may create added stress by counteracting the normal life cycle movement toward individuation. Conversely a geriatric crisis may exaggerate inappropriately a life cycle movement of drawing the family together, resulting in a state of prolonged enmeshment.

The Caregiver and the Family

That families abandon their elderly members is a persistent myth. Studies estimate that the disabled elderly who live in the community receive over 80% of their care from their families. The exceptions are lifelong isolates and the chronically mental ill who constitute 15 to 20% of the population and who receive institutional care in disproportionate numbers. Most older adults have families who help (Lebowitz, 1985). Families relinquish their care of the elderly with difficulty and seek public resources when the financial and emotional burden has become intolerable. Only then do they search out appropriate institutional care. And after institutionalization, family members may experience reactions approaching grief and depression.

A research study by the Andrus Foundation indicates that caregivers of the elderly are primarily spouses who themselves are elderly, whereas adult children are principal caregivers in the absence of a surviving spouse (Survey, 1985). Spouse caregivers are highly vulnerable, being typically older, in poorer health with lower incomes, and the providers of more intensive care for longer periods of time (Montgomery & Datwyler, 1990). The usual pattern of any filial assistance is for adult sons to offer financial aid while daughters provide the hands-on care. As our population ages and there are fewer children per family, almost every woman will need to provide care for an aging parent or parent-in-law. Extended life expectancy, marriage patterns, and differential morbidity by gender mean women will first care for their ill husbands, then for their ailing mothers, in a career of caregiving.

Some women experience pride and an affirmation of family ties, despite financial and personal strain, when they provide loving care to an elder relative. Women, even those with active careers, accept nurturing as their job. This feeling of responsibility may also include a primitive quality, a sense that they must do the nurturing irrespective of the personal cost. Accordingly some women switch to part-time jobs, pass up promotions, or terminate employment altogether—this at a time in our culture when families often depend on two incomes. These women frequently neglect their own needs, and perhaps those of their nuclear family as well. The case of Judy cited in Chapter 2 is an illustration of this inner demand to nurture, which had gone awry and necessitated family treatment. Judy had dropped all other activities and responsibilities to care for her ailing mother, who had finally in ill health expressed appreciation of her daughter. The foci of treatment were a reallocation of roles within the extended family of origin plus some resolution of Judy's grief over a lifetime of alienation from her mother.

An especially vulnerable group are the women over age 55 who are wives and possible caregivers for their ill spouse, who are out-of-home workers, who are parents of young adults, are grandparents, and are caregivers to their own or their husbands' parents. Minority women are another high-risk group of caretakers. Minority elders tend to have lower incomes, poorer housing, and physically demanding jobs. They are thus more likely to have long-term chronic illness (Montgomery & Datwyler, 1990). They need care earlier in the family life cycle and for a longer period of time. Minority elders are more likely to receive the care at home; most minority groups have a lower rate of use of nursing homes. This gives an added dimension to the burden carried by a minority caregiver.

Caregivers need support. Approximately one third of caregivers spend more than 40 hours per week in direct personal care activities (Lebowitz, 1985). Without adequate support, caregivers are at risk of increased depression, anxiety, and failure of their own physical health. Support can be in the form of self-help or mutual aid groups. Men report a need for skill training in the areas of home management and the provision of personal care. Women on the other hand express a need for respite or time for themselves (Lebowitz, 1985). All caregivers need information about normal aging processes as well as the nature and expected course of the family member's illness.

Preventive as well as therapeutic interventions by professionals can be crucial in avoiding or alleviating dysfunctional responses to the burden of care. Each family is unique in its problem-solving methods. Clinicians need to meet with all significant members of the family in order to assess their needs, resources, and risk factors. Human service providers should listen to the family's concerns, help them think of possible solutions, and aid them in choosing what will work best for them. Further intervention is to be provided only if family members cannot successfully use these least intrusive interventions. Studies indicate that group intervention provides social supports while individual intervention produces more effective psychological functioning, and that the combination of both modalities provides better coping with the stress of caregiving (Toseland, Rossiter, Peak, & Smith, 1990).

The clinician should point out to family members, and thus reinforce, any positive dimensions of the family's caregiving. Advantages possibly experienced by the family include "the fulfillment of family obligations, the maintenance of familial responsibilities, the pursuit of moral or religious precepts, and the assurance that care is appropriate and of high quality" (Lebowitz, 1985, p. 458).

Home Care

A study of Americans over age 55 revealed that 84% wished to remain in their present homes for the remainder of their lives (Butler & Lewis, 1982). Home for the elderly is a part of their identity, a place of familiarity with minimal change, a place to maintain a sense of autonomy and control. The concept of home may range from a particular building to the neighborhood in which it is located, to the possessions in the building, to the people living in the home, to neighbors, pets, and plants. It may signify a lifetime dwelling or a more recent location. The meaning of home is individualistic.

Some older adults insist on remaining at home, no matter what the costs of financial security, personal safety, or emotional and physical health. Underlying such persistence may be:

a desire for freedom and independence; a fear of loss of contact with familiar and loved people, places and things; a fear of dying, because of the reputation of hospitals and nursing homes as "houses of death" from which there is no return; and a trepidation about change and the unknown, which frightens people of all ages. (Butler & Lewis, 1982, p. 255)

Communal living is likely viewed by the generation of older adults as a loss of personal freedom.

Conversely not everyone is happy at home. Some older adults dislike their living conditions, even to the extent of being willing to move to an institution. "Home care" needs to be assessed on a person-by-person basis and not automatically embraced as the solution for all elderly, even though families may be ready to make great sacrifices to keep the elder at home. The opinions and wishes of the older adult are essential in this planning process. Nevertheless it is generally accepted that home care is preferable providing that the older adult is not physically dangerous, has no need for inpatient medical care, and an adequate home or a home that can be made adequate is available.

The objectives of home care should be clear in order to plan for needed interventions and services. Is the goal that of rehabilitation, maintenance of current functioning, or support through decline and eventual death? Because of the high rate of change in the lives of the elderly, the objectives and needs for resources should be assessed regularly in order to ensure that they correspond to any improvements or declines in functioning.

Unnecessary dependency and a lowered level of well-being may easily result from unsolicited help and overprotection with coddling. We have already referred to the problem of the overfunctioning and underfunctioning older spouses. Similar dynamics can arise between an elder and other family members and are a signal for professional intervention. Moreover knowing one's limitations for providing help is as vital as knowing one's strengths. This applies to human service providers as well as to family members. If the burden becomes great, seek additional help.

The Decision to Institutionalize

Families come to the decision to institutionalize with great difficulty and after stress has become unbearable. Yet modern society tends to blame families for increasing the drain on public resources should a member be placed in a Medicaid- or Medicare-funded nursing home or institution. This climate serves to compound whatever guilt and sorrow the family may already experience regarding their decision.

When to place a relative in a nursing home or other institution has no universal answer. Many families hold out until problems such as wandering, with a need for continuous supervision, or incontinence, with a need for nursing services, become severe and signal the exhaustion of familial resources. Other families use community resources to the fullest to supplement their own capabilities and institutionalize only when medical problems require hospitalization. Hospice care has given many older adults the opportunity to choose the surroundings in which they will die. Yet at times the decision for institutionalization is made and it is often fraught with feelings of guilt and abandonment. Adult daughters, so frequently the caregivers, are especially affected by this stressful decision.

Families of an institutionalized member present the institution with several issues. Family members experience stress from having made the decision. They also are concerned about the quality of care given their family member, including medical or psychiatric care, and the quality of the relative's life in the institution. Family therapy is appropriate for addressing the family's expectations for the relative's level of functioning in the institution, the roles of the family members themselves in relation to the institution, and the new roles in the outside world once the relative has been institutionalized.

A preliminary step to making decisions regarding institutionalization is the recognition of clues for determining when parents need help. Family members should have information about those clues. Unpaid bills, bounced checks, moldy food in the refrigerator, unfilled prescriptions, overdrawn bank accounts, a decrease in the elder's ability to walk or eat or dress him or herself—these are some signals that the elder member needs monitoring. The capacity for independent living, or for semi-independent living in another's home should be assessed at this point. The decrease in control over daily living skills may be transient and treatable. It may be caused by an adverse reaction to a medication, a medical condition (such as a thyroid problem, pneumonia, or anemia), a nutritional imbalance or deficit, or a psychological problem such as depression. When a lessening of functioning persists, it should neither be attributed to aging nor be presumed to be irreversible. It warrants full medical assessment.

Elders may resist such an assessment for fear that the results will be used to force them into a nursing home for life. From similar fears, spouses may cover up for each other, and problems may be undetected for years. Changes in functioning may also be gradual and thus go unnoticed by the spouse or companion. The more isolated the elder, the more likely the problems will remain hidden until a crisis occurs and the police are called. Whatever the course of discovery, elders need clear assurance from family members and clinicians that these people are not trying to usurp the elder's independence. This goal is best achieved when the older adult is part of the problem-solving process at the earliest point of recognition of persisting trouble. Clinicians will meet varying amounts of reluctance by the family to include their elder members in this process. Considerable creativity may be required to identify the more available family members and bring them into the planning of care. It is not unusual for interventions of second-order change, presented in Chapter 4, to be indicated in such instances.

Families may be confused and need education regarding the meaning of some changes in their elder member's behavior (Tilley, 1990). For instance, they need to learn that physical complaints may serve as a request for attention or support and thus the realities need to be clarified. Rigid behavior may be an attempt to avoid or reduce further change. Childlike behavior may be a way to seek times when life was easier, as a result of stress. Extreme dependency may represent a fear of failure. Denial of current limits and needs may be a statement that the person feels unable to manage these changes. Confabulation, or making up information, may be a cover-up for memory loss. Projection of the cause of the elder's own troubles onto another may stem from a reluctance to accept one's failings, finding it easier to blame another than to admit a decrease in functioning. Paranoia or extreme suspiciousness, which may result from isolation or a breakdown in support, frequently is associated with auditory or visual loss. The gaps in reality that ensue may be filled with misconceptions as the person tries to make sense of the environment. Suspiciousness as an attempt to maintain personal safety needs to be separated from that due to loss. These possibilities for misunderstanding an elder's behavior are prime targets for family intervention.

When at all possible, family members while healthy and alert should be encouraged to think through and share with trusted others what elements of long-term care are important to them. How vital is it to remain in one's own community? What elements of life-style are most valued? What resources, both residential and financial, are available? A living will stating one's wishes in case of becoming incapacitated and other legal documents providing for one's medical, legal, and/or financial affairs should be considered. Health insurance is a primary concern. Human service providers should have available to them a referral network composed of professionals knowledgeable and responsible in these areas, for referral of families needing assistance in planning.

Resistance by older adults and their families to wise planning for older years should be recognized by clinicians as a likely denial of the realities of aging. Families should be confronted about this avoidance and helped to identify the basis from which it stems, perhaps through intergenerational histories, reminiscences, or exploration and resolution of previous deaths and losses.

Elderly Parents as Caregivers for Adult Dependent Children

As life expectancies and medical care have increased, people live both longer and with chronic illness. A group of neglected families is those in which elderly parents are the primary caregivers for dependent adult children. These elderly parents live in "perpetual parenthood" (Jennings, 1987, p. 430). Their stress increases markedly as their own aging process becomes paramount and declining physical abilities begin to limit their capacity for giving care. The question of who will provide care to the dependent adult child after the elderly parents' deaths is crucial. Many disabled adults, especially those who are developmentally disabled, outlive their parents. Added to this concern is that of the elders' own care and the source of its provision. If one elder parent is still able, will that parent be caregiver for the frail spouse plus the disabled adult child, or will family members assist? Isolation has likely been a pattern in these parents' lives, a pattern not easily broken. One study with implications for intergenerational caregiving (Soldo & Myllyluoma, 1983) indicated that when an older couple lives with another person, the couple was disabled and so was the "other." Moreover the other care receiver most frequently was an impaired child of the elderly couple.

These elderly parents may well need counseling to plan for their own care as they age. The lifetime burden of supporting a handicapped offspring as a child, then an adult, may have limited the parents' vocational advancement while draining their financial resources, leaving little for their own retirement. Furthermore the care of their adult child after their deaths should be made a priority as well. Mobilizing resources for each generation becomes additionally compelling because of the family's long experience of isolation.

The clinician should supportively but persistently confront any denial of the parents' need to face the issue of the care of their aging dependent child. All extended family members should be considered as possible sources of support and should become engaged in the family sessions. They likely will need reassurance from the clinician that the goal of the sessions is not to overburden anyone, including those who may have stayed away in the past from such a fear.

Further Aspects of Treatment

The family's response to the illness or decline of an aging member is pivotal to the welfare of the older member as well as to the general functioning of the family. If the elder holds roles crucial for the maintenance of the family system, the structure and role distribution of the family will change in important ways. Most likely the family will need to assume the added tasks of coordinating the services that support family functioning.

Therapeutic interventions for families unable to manage the changes and related stress may concentrate on the ecological environment, the family of origin, and various aspects of family structure and process. A genogram concentrating upon chronic illness, major health problems, and medical causes of death may be used to highlight familial patterns of caregiving and responses to geriatric crises or needs. Circular questioning, an intervention presented in Chapter 4, can be useful to ferret out instances of suspected secondary gain from a debilitating condition as well as those instances of the patient's role serving as a solution to another problem. Questions could explore variables before and after the onset of the disability. Other questions could ask hypothetically what might happen should the care receiver begin to function more fully. If the family sustains a steadfast investment in maintaining an illness, the family therapist should consider using indirect interventions. The clinician might identify and reframe positively the advantages of the illness for the family, praise the selflessness of the handicapped elder, and warn the family against changing too rapidly. The human service provider needs to be alert to possibilities of being co-opted into the family system in such situations, that is, of colluding with the family by overfocusing upon the medical condition or frailty.

When an elder member is afflicted with senile dementia, adult members should prepare not only themselves but also the children in the family for the irritability, childishness, and confusion that the grandparent eventually will display. This preparation is essential for minimizing the elder's isolation and the grandchild's trauma. Families need education about handling such matters. Otherwise they may mistakenly refrain from discussing the changes in the elder's behavior until they can show no emotion while doing so. Or they may attempt to hide the truth from children instead of explaining the changes in a context that relates the elder's behavior to the illness and not to a reduction of love.

If at all possible, children should be allowed to visit their elder relatives, a practice that maintains the social contact and may even ameliorate the elder's disability. During these visits, the children can ask about the past of the elder relative whose long-term memory may still be intact. This sharing serves to strengthen the child's sense of identity and continuity with the past, while giving the elder some advantages of reminiscence. The reduction in the elder's social isolation is a preventative step toward warding off depression.

DEPRESSION AND SUICIDE

Depression is the most common of emotional illnesses found in older people. It accounts for nearly 50% of the psychiatric hospitalizations for this age group (McQuellon & Reifler, 1989). Suicide is one of the 10 leading causes of death in the United States. The highest rate of all groups is for white males in their 80s (Butler & Lewis, 1982).

Depression

Depression mounts in degree and frequency with old age as a corollary to the increased loss of much that is emotionally valued by the older adult (Butler & Lewis, 1982). The depressed retiree has already been discussed. Depression may also accompany other disorders such as organic brain diseases. Depression often is associated with physical illness that is painful and/or incapacitating, and is a common accompaniment to hearing loss. Depression in those who are dying may be so profound that they are avoided by their family and friends, who feel their own helplessness to change the situation. Another prominent cause of depression among the elderly is substance abuse. This issue is addressed later in this chapter.

There is some evidence that, with age, depression lessens in intensity but increases in physical manifestations (Butler & Lewis, 1982). Symptoms of depression include insomnia, despair, lethargy, anorexia, loss of interest, and somatic complaints. The symptoms of depression may be more or less obvious. They often are reversible. Therefore a medical assessment is essential for treatment planning. Unfortunately practitioners and family members mistakenly may believe that treatment for depression accompanying physical or organic disorders might be too much for the older adult to manage.

A myth attributes depression to the normal process of aging. Depression can also be misdiagnosed as senility. And this generation of older adults is for the most part reluctant to seek mental health care. In summary, the depressed elderly are undertreated.

The course of depression in the elderly may be sequential (McQuellon & Reifler, 1989). Its first evidence may be at the time of bodily changes such as a sensory loss. The biological changes, increasing disability, and a new sense of helplessness are issues for the elderly that may set the stage for the onset of depression. These developmental factors then interact with the older adult's special weaknesses or vulnerabilities that are highly sensitive to the pressures of aging. Factors of vulnerability include neurotransmission, cognitive functioning, ego functioning, and external support systems. Precipitating events may interact with these variables, leading to the depression. Interventions of family therapy are appropriate at any point in this sequence: at the onset when biological changes first become evident, in relation to the support systems that are a factor in the elder's vulnerabilities, and for resolution of any precipitating event. Such therapeutic steps have as their two goals the avoidance or alleviation of the elder's depression and education and guidance of the family in order to support the aging process in a positive fashion. If left untreated, the depression could lead to clinical results, such as the elder's helpless behavior or suicide, and to social consequences, such as disrupted or destructive relationships with family members and other caregivers.

Of course the elderly may have been depressed prior to their later years and may, like any segment of the population, experience any of the various clinical forms of depression. Human service providers should be familiar with the features and treatment of neurotic or dysthymic depression, bipolar or manic-depressive disorder, and psychotic or major depression. Symptoms of major depression in the elderly may be different from those in younger patients. As we noted, there is a predominance of somatic complaints; they may mask the more typical depressive symptoms. For milder depressions associated with a sense of personal insignificance, the older adult needs help finding new roles and activities of genuine interest. Physical exercise and talking about the problems can be helpful. More serious depressions, related to grave illness, death of a loved one, or other losses, may require medical measures such as medication in addition to skilled family therapy that includes some individual sessions. The release of anger and guilt in therapy sessions can be especially valuable.

Most families can tolerate short periods of sadness in their family members, but find it wearing when the older adult is depressed and severely withdrawn. Systems theory posits the mutuality of depression within a family. The relationships in which the depressed elder is a participant may be a cause or a consequence of that depression. Thus a caregiver of a depressed elder is at risk of becoming depressed.

Therefore family interventions are indicated whenever assistance is sought for depression, whether it is by the depressed older adult, the caregiver, or another concerned or depressed family member. Family sessions can reduce the risk of misguided help consisting of a sequence of reassurance, advice, direction, coercion, and attack, and finally rejection. Involvement of the elder's spouse in therapy provides several benefits. It helps mitigate the risk of relapse by the depressed older adult. It lowers the risk of the spouse developing depression or another psychological disturbance. Finally the spouse's involvement in the treatment lessens the chance of other family members becoming dysfunctional in their relationships with the elder and each other. When providing counseling to the depressed older adult and the family, reframing of the depression can be helpful to empower those involved. Making the problem solvable would emphasize moving slowly in treatment and tackling the issue in small steps without having to solve what is not solvable. A positive reframe would present the situation as one that is manageable and a challenge, not a threat. Inactivity would be given a positive connotation; the clinician would acknowledge the reality of the depression and the presence of problems while defining the family's efforts as positive ones that have backfired, have been unrecognized, or were misunderstood.

Above all an effective therapist recognizes that the life circumstances of a disabled older adult, particularly one in an institution, realistically may be depressing. The afflicted elders and their families need clinicians who neither deny nor overreact. This requirement usually means the clinician has resolved most personal issues about depression in the elderly.

Suicide

Suicidal threats of older adults should be taken seriously. Those attempting suicide are more likely to fail if they are below age 35, and more likely to succeed if over 50. Seldom does a person over age 65 fail in an attempt. Men generally are more successful than women in committing suicide. In fact suicidal threats by the elderly are a rarity; older adults simply kill themselves (Butler & Lewis, 1982).

Suicides can be abrupt or drawn out over long periods of time. The elderly use the same methods of quick death as other age groups, with shooting themselves being a primary means. Forms of extended self-destruction include not eating, not taking medicine, alcoholism, delaying treatment, and taking excessive risks. This long-term, or subintentional, process of self-inflicted death is not included in the statistics of suicide, which recognize suicide only as a single act.

Whenever depression is detected in an older adult, the potential for suicide should be assessed immediately and thoroughly. Following are clues indicating the need for an evaluation of suicidal potential (Butler & Lewis, 1982):

Depression with no outlet for anger
Withdrawal
Bereavement (especially in the first year of loss)
Isolation
Expectation of own death from some cause
Decrease in the organization and complexity of behavior
Increased helplessness
Institutionalization
Physical illness
Alcoholism
Desire and rational decisions to protect others from financial disaster
Philosophical decisions of no more pleasure or purpose in life
Decreased self-regard
Meaninglessness of life

Organic mental deterioration

Nightmares and changes in sleep patterns

Being a white male

Of course, verbal remarks about "ending it all" or "others would be better off without me" should be given full attention.

The high risk of suicide for older males has been hypothesized to correlate with women's lifelong experience of passivity, suggestibility, and malleability, which translate into adaptability for survival. Older white men in our society have more status to lose as they decline in power and influence with age. A lesser status is not new in the lives of African-Americans; thus their status does not drop as much in old age and may even rise.

Old age needs to offer something to live for. The extent of family relationships, friendships, interests, activities, and sense of one's usefulness are predictors of survival in originally healthy older adults. Families play vital roles in the maintenance of healthy functioning for their elder members. They must be an integral part of any intervention when suicide or depression are present.

Clinicians should choose therapeutic interventions carefully if any evidence of suicidal potential is revealed. We wish to reiterate here our former warning. Indirect interventions that prescribe a behavior should not be used for changing behaviors physically dangerous to self or others. This includes behaviors with suicidal implications.

SUBSTANCE ABUSE

The use of drugs, including alcohol, is considered abuse if the person persists with a particular pattern of use despite negative consequences for self or others. Because people generally alter a behavior if it brings negative results, the concept of addiction helps account for the inexplicable persistence of this negative behavior.

Elders' substance abuse often is not recognized by family members or helping professionals. And when it is diagnosed, it may not be addressed. Estimates of the prevalence of alcoholism among older adults vary from 2 to 20%, with significantly higher representation among medical and psychiatric patients as well as nursing home residents. It is probable that the rates of elders' alcohol abuse are similar to those of younger adults. It also appears that about one third of older alcoholics are late-onset; that is, they did not drink or their drinking was not problematic until after age 60. In addition elders are at risk for developing a dependence upon psychotropic medication. Their access to such medications is greatly enhanced at a time when both their life stresses and their isolation may be increasing. Older adults are less likely than younger adults to use "street drugs," although there are occasional instances of the use of marijuana and abuse of cocaine. As they age, many elders appear to switch to alcohol or to cheaper, legal, and now more accessible prescription drugs.

Family systems theory is a particularly useful viewpoint for considering substance abuse among older adults, because the initial psychological crisis often occurs in an adult child or helper of the abuser. Given the nature of addiction, others in the social system that includes the abuser typically are pained and seek help before the abuser. The problem of the abuse may not be identified as such. Therefore the therapist's initial task is twofold. First the addiction must be identified as part of the problem. Then, as well, person(s) in a relationship with the abuser need to receive information regarding the nature of addiction as well as the choices available to them.

Case Example

A 48-year-old woman, Ms. Sampson, had built a small home on her rural property for her father. Mr. Sampson, a chronic alcoholic, was showing increasingly irresponsible and frightening behavior. She checked on him several times each day to make sure he was not in trouble. To keep him off the roads, she supplied him with liquor, although it turns out that he had another source as well. She also cooked his meals, took him to doctors, and provided a general taxi service for him. She became increasingly depressed and was prescribed antidepressants by her and her father's physician. Ms. Sampson continued to postpone recommended surgery, at some personal peril, because she was afraid of what might happen to her father. Later, upon a friend's urging, she sought counseling and through her therapist contacted a chemical dependency program. After several weeks of treatment that included education about addiction and its effect on family members, she decided to have the surgery. She told her father that he could not stay in the house while she was gone unless he obtained treatment and stayed sober. Otherwise she would help him find an adult foster care home where he could stay while she had the surgery and recuperated. Her father agreed to enter treatment and stayed sober for at least the two years he was in contact with the agency.

Obstacles to Identification of the Problem

The first step in intervening in a pattern of substance abuse is, of course, to identify the abuse. A number of obstacles make this a difficult task in working with older adults. Foremost is the general lack of information about the symptoms of substance abuse in older adults. The reader is referred to Haugland (1989) or Schuckit (1990) for information on diagnosis. Many of the symptoms of substance abuse—changes in memory, lack of coordination, deteriorating self-care, isolation, depressed mood—are often interpreted as "symptoms" of aging itself and are not investigated further. Both the family and helpers often subscribe to the myth of aging that claims substance use is "understandable" and should not be withheld from the older adult, given the inevitable bleakness and painfulness of old age. This belief may be complemented by the equally ageist and false belief that older adults cannot recover from substance abuse, that is, they are too old to learn new ways of coping. Finally adult children of alcoholics may be well trained to ignore signs of substance abuse, especially early onset substance abuse, or to explain away the related problems. These denying adults include not only the abuser's own children but also the overly represented group of helping professionals who grew up with substance abuse in their families.

The Context of Abuse

While younger adults may well come to the attention of clinicians by virtue of the legal or occupational effects of their use-related behavior, the substance abuse of older adults is more likely identified following a medical or family crisis. Because it is difficult to maintain a substance abusing life style without help, it is generally reasonable to assume that an abuser has an "enabling" system. In such a system, family, friends, or helping professionals cushion the abuser from experiencing the effects of the abuse. The enablers assume responsibilities as the abuser becomes more irresponsible. They act to reduce the pain and to solve problems resulting from the abuser's use.

Precipitating Crises

A crisis for the system is likely to occur when there is a change in the enabling system. Examples of such changes include the following: the enabling spouse has a medical crisis of his or her own; an adult child who is playing a central role moves away or assumes other tasks at work or within his or her own nuclear family; or, a helping professional, especially a longtime physician, retires or moves on. Any of these transitions can manifest itself as a crisis for a middle-aged adult child who then becomes stressed and conflicted about the increased demands from, and the deteriorating condition of, the abuser.

The other common precipitant of crisis occurs when the demands and needs of the abuser move beyond the capacity of the enabling system. This often occurs when some medical complication—frequently a symptom of, or at least exacerbated by, the substance abuse—requires outside medical intervention. At this juncture medical personnel have the opportunity to disrupt the usual patterns of behavior. They can reframe the nature of the problem by recognizing and clarifying the central relationship of the substance abuse to the presenting health and life problems. In turn the possible solutions to the medical complication can be cast in terms of abstinence and "disenabling."

Case Example

The following example from practice illustrates an alcoholic's needs exceeding the capacity of the enabling system. Mr. Chase, 76 years of age, had several "girlfriends," including his ex-wife, who took care of him. Mr. Chase was charming when not incapacitated by alcohol. Consequently four women came by his house and supplied him with alcohol, shopped for and made his meals, and even bathed and cleansed him as he became weaker and less able to care for himself. In time Mr. Chase became essentially bedridden, with barely enough strength and coordination to manage his most basic personal needs. This process was of several years' duration and ended only when Mr. Chase became obviously jaundiced and clearly "sick." He refused to go to a doctor, but one of the women sought medical help. The doctor brought together three of the four enabling women and explored with them the possibility that being less helpful might be more helpful. The women agreed to contact the other suppliers of alcohol and to cut off Mr. Chase's supply. He had previously experienced one painful withdrawal at home and now readily entered the hospital to avoid a repeat and to obtain medical help with the detoxification.

Given the nature of addiction, there is a good possibility that a substance abuser will not willingly recognize substance use as part of the problem. The clinician in that case should focus on disrupting whatever system facilitates the abuse. The family therapist engages family members and other helpers in clarifying the role of substances in the ongoing painful process and in redefining what is helpful in this context. Family members may then become less ready to compensate for or smooth over the difficulties that arise from substance use. This change involves behavioral shifts as simple as no longer buying and supplying alcohol to the abuser, or involves more drastic measures such as a spouse separating from or divorcing the abuser.

The clinician's role, of course, is not to tell family members and enablers how they should behave. Instead the therapist should help clarify with them the effects of their actions and explore how those actions mesh with their own needs, goals, and values.

Complexities of "Enabling" With Older Adult Substance Abusers

Older adult substance abusers often pose a difficult set of issues. What are the older adult's needs that arise from the ongoing substance use, and what are needs that would have been present even in sobriety? The working assumption in relation to younger substance abusers in family-focused therapy is generally that the abusers could be responsible for themselves and self-sufficient if they were sober. Some older adults, however, even in sobriety, may need help in areas such as self-care and transportation. It may seem unfair and dangerous to family members to withdraw too much from the older abuser.

The balance between what is unhelpful and "enabling" and what is essential care is often unclear. An abusing elder with compromised health poses a dilemma for family and nonfamily "enablers." Because substance abuse is clearly damaging to the person's health and will almost certainly shorten and diminish the quality of his or her life, family members and helpers may want to stop supporting the abuse. Yet at the same time they may fear both the consequences of and the reduction of their enabling behavior. Will the abuser survive experiencing more fully the consequences of his or her abuse? This is an issue regardless of the substance abuser's age. There may be less margin, however, for older adults who, even barring a cataclysmic accident, may not survive decreased enabling.

Respectful Recognition of the Benefits of Substance Use for All Family Members

It is critical that all family members, and perhaps nonfamily helpers as well, be cognizant and respectful of the perceived benefits of the substance use and the fears related to the loss of the substance(s). The series of crises that characterize the substance use over time may have served to organize family life, define levels of engagement and closeness, and delineate and support roles within the family. The substance abuse may bring adult children into regular contact with their parents and at the same time limit the demands for intimacy during this contact. For the abuser, being intoxicated already limits the capacity for emotional closeness; for all family members, the focus on the abuser's problems provides a ready distraction from getting too close. Other personal and emotional issues, as well as relationship issues involving other family members, may remain submerged as long as the ongoing crises of the abuser continue. Family members, including the abuser, may greatly fear the loss of the rituals of gathering that the abuse provides. They also may fear the lack of distraction from other feelings and issues that have been kept at bay by the dominating affect of the ongoing abuse. Part of recovery for the family is to develop alternative methods of convening and regulating emotional distance that do not rely upon abuse.

Motivating the Abuser to Address the Substance Abuse

Many of the issues mentioned above may be addressed without the older adult being present. Moreover if the older adult does not share the family members' perception of the nature of the substance abuse problem, the family may proceed to reduce enabling by staging an intervention (Johnson, 1986). An intervention is a method wherein a group of people important to the abuser gather and, after education and rehearsal, confront the abuser. In a calm manner they share specific recollections of their painful experiences of the person's abuse. The group then suggests to the abuser a prearranged course of action that includes entering treatment. If the abuser refuses the proposal, each group member then describes how his or her relationship with the abuser will deteriorate if the treatment continues to be refused.

Nonfamily Enablers and the Therapeutic Contract

The role of nonfamily helpers within the enabling system and, in turn, in therapy, may complicate work with older adults. This is especially true because substance-abusing elders typically are dependent upon others for basic self-care. Nonfamily helpers working through either geriatric or more broad-based agencies that offer home-based help for the elderly may assume more and more responsibility for the everyday tasks of the older adult. In this process they may serve as suppliers for alcohol, perhaps as part of the shopping that they do for food. They may help procure sedatives for their charges and support their use without medical supervision. They may support the abuser's notion that nothing is wrong, or at least that use is not a central part of any problem, either by not confronting what they see or by supporting or creating an alternate explanation for events. The worker or the agency also may be the referral source for the abuser entering treatment or may oppose any such referral. Either way the question that arises is: What is the nature of the therapeutic contract with nonfamily helpers?

Case Example

Mr. Robinson, an alcoholic in his 70s, was referred to an inpatient program for chemical dependency treatment by a home health-care agency that had supported and supervised him and his invalid wife since Mr. Robinson's retirement. While earlier in life he had encountered some problems with drinking, since retirement he steadily increased his alcohol consumption. As he gradually became less responsible for his needs, the agency workers began to assume more and more of his responsibilities in much the same way that family members do. At the time of referral these human service providers were balancing his checkbook, paying his bills, doing his taxes, and buying his groceries, including much of his alcohol. As he drank more, they allowed his increasingly abusive behavior toward his wife to go unchallenged. Mr. Robinson later became aware that, after a lifetime of counterdependency, he had "given in" to being cared for. Meanwhile, during his hospital stay, he made numerous phone calls to the agency with complaints about his care—complaints that indicated he felt very anxious. Several agency workers responded by protecting him from staff in a manner that amplified Mr. Robinson's anxiety and diffused the focus of treatment. These dynamics are not restricted to nonfamily helpers but can apply as well to family members.

Clinicians often assume they have an implicit contract to ask questions for assessment and to comment upon, even confront, family members' behavior relative to continued abuse or recovery. Generally this is a shared assumption; family members perceive such behavior of the therapist as being appropriate. Nonfamily helping professionals or paraprofessionals, however, may not accept "scrutiny" or "criticism" of their behavior by the clinician as being appropriate. They may angrily disengage from, not support, or actively undermine the treatment. They may also stop referring to the treatment program or practice. It is therefore helpful early in the referral process for the clinician and the nonfamily helper to have a dialogue about the nature of the contract and the relevant clinical issues. This step facilitates the overt, mutual definition of the contract. Because the role and attitudes of nonfamily helpers are often critical to the abuser's recovery, it is important to engage these professionals in the therapy in a clearly defined way.

Dealing With the Past and Engagement in the Present

One family issue important for recovery involves addressing past pain and hurt that stem from interactions during intoxication, and the possible reinvolvement of the emotionally more distant adult children. Depending upon the drinking behavior of the abuser and the length of the abuse, some or even many memories of painful encounters and hurtful exchanges between the substance abuser and other family members are likely. As treatment progresses and the focus shifts from the need to take care of the abuser, the abuser begins to take better care of himself or herself, and the family members begin to focus more on themselves. This shift is often accompanied by an upsurge of family members' anger and resentment, of which they had been unaware. The first year of sobriety is the most likely time for a divorce.

Although no hard data seems to be available on this topic, practice indicates that this time is also one of high risk for children being emotionally, or even physically, alienated from the abuser. Especially if the children are long suffering and "heroically" helpful does this hazard seem probable.

Addressing the resentments is an important aspect of therapy. One caveat, however, is to avoid making this step an all-or-nothing type of encounter that could perpetuate the substance abuse style of addressing discomfort in an inefficient and overly dramatic manner. During the course of an older adult's substance abuse, it is common for the children to take different, polarized positions relative to the abuser. On the one hand some children may remain exceptionally involved and play regular caretaking roles that support denial. On the other hand some children may have pulled away and kept a wary distance from their parents. It is the distant children who may be more open to reengagement with the abuser upon sobriety, and who will be welcomed by the parents with open arms. Interacting with the returning children may seem easier; it entails less burden of sharing the resentment-saturated memories of the roller coaster of the recent years with the substance abuser. The heroically helpful children, though, may feel great resentment that their prodigal siblings enjoy such unfair favor now, during the good times.

Treatment Choices

Many older adults need some medical support while withdrawing from alcohol or medications. A medical assessment by a physician knowledgeable about substance abuse is a critical part of the treatment. This applies even to the treatment of late-onset abusers of modest amounts of substances. It is poor practice, and legally dangerous, for nonmedical personnel to neglect to obtain medical input.

For many clients, inpatient treatment is indicated as a first step. The older adult's ongoing involvement in a therapy group focused on substance abuse, as well as participation in a 12-step group, may be crucial adjuncts to ongoing couples or family therapy during inpatient or later outpatient treatment.

It is important to keep in mind that recovery is an individualized process. The course of therapy with any substance abuser and his or her family could assume any of the facets described in other sections of this book. The range of potential recovery issues is all inclusive.

ELDER ABUSE

Statistics from the U.S. Department of Justice for 1988 show that older adults are the least frequent victims of crime; that is, of reported crimes. Mistreatment of the elderly is frequently not reported. The House Select Committee on Aging projected in its 1990 report that 1.5 million elderly Americans, or 5% of all older Americans, are abused each year, with only about one in every eight cases reported. This is a 50% increase in the past 10 years. Elder abuse is one of the unspoken and unaddressed issues of contemporary society. One hears the comment that it is better left alone, because what would we do with the people if we knew they needed services or a place to stay, a shelter? This is the rationale for doing nothing, or very little, that kept child abuse hidden much too long. It took extensive education and the development of the awareness of social workers, teachers, the police, lawyers, prosecutors, judges, and our society in general before programs were developed to help the survivors of child abuse and their families. In many ways it seems we are at the same starting point for elder abuse.

Who Are the Abused and Their Abusers?

The same U.S. Department of Justice report stated that victims of elder abuse are likely to be 75 years of age or older. They are in poor health. They live with someone else upon whom they are dependent for their basic needs. In some instances they have a mental or physical impairment.

A highly acclaimed study of over 2,000 elderly (Pillemer & Finkelhor, 1988) contradicted the myth that the abuse of noninstitutionalized elderly is perpetrated by the caretaking son or daughter who becomes exhausted and unthinkingly lashes out at the elderly. Only 23% of the abused elderly in the study were maltreated by an adult child, whereas 65% had been abused by the spouse. This means that frequently elder abuse is to be likened to spouse abuse. And spouse abuse is underreported, although it now is beginning to receive the attention it deserves.

Elders of both genders are at risk of being abused. The 1990 U.S. Department of Justice report stated that women are more likely to be abused, which supports the prevailing belief. In the Pillemer and Finkelhor study, however, elderly male spouses were twice as likely to be abused as female spouses, although female spouses reported more serious injuries when abused. Abuse was present at all economic levels and in all age groups of the elderly in the Pillemer and Finkelhor study (1988).

Abusers are usually in the caretaker role. They are also dependent upon the recipient of their care for assistance with such needs as finances, housing, transportation, cooking, and cleaning. Thus the dependency may be mutual. The abusers themselves likely have experienced recent stressful life events, such as illness or the death of a loved one. They frequently have a mental or emotional problem. Abusers themselves may have been abused as a child by the person they now victimize, or were abused earlier by the spouse who now is abused in retaliation. However, this theory has not yet been substantiated by research studies.

Substance abuse is often implicated in elder abuse. This picture is quite different from the prevailing view that the older adult has become too heavy a burden to well-meaning relatives who just cannot cope any longer and therefore become abusive. That view is one that blames the victim. Although caretaker stress is a significant variable in elder abuse, it must not be assumed to be the only or even the predominant factor.

Types of Abuse

The various forms of abuse usually included in any discussion are physical abuse, financial abuse or exploitation, psychological abuse, neglect, and violation of rights. We do not include self abuse in our discussion of elder abuse.

Physical abuse includes the range of shoving, pushing, or grabbing to slapping, kicking, beating, throwing objects, sexual abuse, and rape. It is any abuse causing welts, sprains, burns, bruises, dislocation of joints, or broken bones. It is any action leading to injury or death.

Financial abuse means mismanaging money or stealing property, savings, credit cards, or Social Security checks. It includes forcing an elder to sign documents such as a will or to transfer ownership of stocks, bonds, or savings. It is the illegal or unethical exploitation or use of another's property, funds, or assets.

Psychological abuse involves verbal harassment, threats, insults, name-calling, humiliation, intimidation, isolation, infantilization or treatment as a child, or withholding companionship. It is the infliction of mental anguish.

Neglect means the failure to fulfill a caretaking responsibility, to give medicine, food, or personal care. Active neglect includes willful, conscious attempts to cause stress or injury for the elder, such as abandonment or denial of food, medical care, dentures, or eyeglasses. Passive neglect infers an inability on the part of the caretaker to realize what care is needed for the elder or to carry out the necessary tasks. In most instances passive neglect is a tragic result of well-meaning family members or other caretakers who are incapable of meeting the elder's needs.

Violation of rights refers to such acts as confinement of the elder unreasonably or against the person's will, forcing the elder out of the home, or other forms of control of the elder's behavior.

Verbal aggression, physical violence, and neglect were the most frequent forms of abuse found in the Pillemer and Finkelhor study. The House Select Committee on Aging cited physical violence and financial abuse as the most common types of elder abuse, followed by the denial of basic human rights and psychological abuse. As elder abuse is reported more accurately in the future, the relative incidence of the various types may shift.

Clues to Elder Abuse

Some signs and symptoms of elder mistreatment (Douglass, 1987) that are found in the abusing caregiver are:

New self-neglect, conflicting stories, mounting resentment, excusing failure, shifting blame, aggressive/defensive behavior, substance abuse, unusual fatigue, new affluence, new health problems, preoccupation/depression,
and withholding food/medication.

The clues to elder abuse that may be detected in the recipient of abusive
care are:

Increasing depression, anxiety, withdrawal/timidity, hostility, unrespon-
siveness, confusion, physical injury, new poverty, longing for death,
vague health complaints, anxiety to please, and shopping for medical care.

These are the most prevalent symptoms and signs. It is not a complete
list, as abuse may exist even in the absence of the above clues. Nor does
the presence of any particular indicator guarantee that abuse is present,
but it is compelling evidence of the need to explore the possibility. If
an indicator increases in frequency or severity, surely the possibility of
abuse should be investigated.

Continued Abuse

Abuse continues for several reasons, one of which is from fear and
shame. The fear of retaliation or of what will happen to the victims if
they tell are strong deterrents to change. Some abused elders are silent
from a wish to protect the abuser and the extended family from shame.
And the abused elder may experience personal shame from allowing the
abuse to happen or from being helpless to end it. Denial of the abuse
may be an attempt to live with the reality.

Another reason for continued abuse is the elder's dependence upon
the abuser. The victim may be unaware of resources available for help.
Part of this perception is based in grim reality, as few communities have
respite shelters. Many domestic violence shelters will not accept bat-
tered elders. Social isolation of the family and/or the elder may not only
prevent detection of the abuse, but also it makes escape especially
difficult. It is a significant factor in the continuance of elder abuse.

Prevention

For comprehensive and practical guidelines for the prevention of
elder abuse, for both the family and its elder member, we refer the reader
to Appendix E. In this excellent reference, Douglass (1987, pp. 25-29)

addresses many of the previously noted risk factors that should be understood by all human service providers working with the elderly and their families.

Therapists should pay attention to the relative physical strength of the men and women in a family at risk of elder abuse. This ratio, as well as the impact of any intimidation or previous incident of physical abuse, no matter how long ago, may serve as a regulator of the balance of power between the couple.

Because the elderly seek help from the police for social problems as well as for those caused by crime, programs to educate the police in the detection of elder abuse could provide a major step in its prevention. If a human service provider suspects elder abuse has occurred, the professional should be prepared to give the following information when contacting the police or another authority:

- Name and location of victim
- Need for any immediate medical care, if any
- Presence of suspected abuser, or likeliness of abuser's return
- Name and location of person reporting
- Summary of what abuse occurred
- What assistance the reporter is requesting
- Evidence for need of a check of suspected victim's welfare, if any (unusual noises or smells coming from the home, uncollected mail or newspapers, no response to phone or doorbell, refusal of entrance of caregiver, missed appointments, inability to contact the suspected victim)

Issues of Treatment

Before any treatment plan is formalized, the human service provider should determine any past history of attempts at treatment for abuse of the older adult. Is there more than one abuser, such as the husband and the son? Did any strategies prove successful in the past, perhaps regarding some aspect of the abuse, or regarding a particular abuser, that might be useful now? Were previous strategies unsuccessful, and if so, why?

Treatment for the Abused

The treatment of the survivor of elder abuse has been conceptualized as being in three stages (Breckman & Adelman, 1988). They are reluctance, recognition, and rebuilding. These stages assist the survivor from a point in life that entails mistreatment to a point in life without it. The model is based upon the degree of the survivor's receptivity to help.

The reluctance stage is characterized by the survivor's tendency toward self-blame for the abuse, perhaps excusing or protecting the abuser. The survivor may even seek assistance for the abuser rather than for him or herself. Breckman and Adelman (1988) report that the more frequent and severe the mistreatment, the stronger the abused person's focus will be upon obtaining help for the abuser. Of course both the abused and the abuser need treatment, but the survivor at this stage may be aware of only half the picture. The abused elder is usually still isolated from friends and family members. The less the contact with others, the more the contact with the abuser is valued and the reality of the situation is skewed.

The recognition stage involves a widening view of the abuse. The survivor begins to understand the complexity of the abusive situation and to realize that help is necessary. Denial and self-blame lessen as self-acceptance gains worth and notice. The survivor can now more easily discuss the abuse and accompanying concerns with family members, friends, and support group participants. Isolation becomes less of a factor. As they begin to talk with others, survivors may fear retaliation by the abuser, and indeed the abuser may attempt to prevent contact between the victimized elder and the external world. Nevertheless, this stage is marked by an interest in reaching out to others, accompanied by some efforts to do so.

Rebuilding as a stage is the period of reshaping the survivor's identity and building a life style that does not include abuse. Survivors are now willing to terminate the connection with an abusive family member or caretaker. They no longer believe they are responsible for the abusing family member's happiness or that they must tolerate mistreatment. They have a supportive network available to them. The abuser may continue to threaten the survivor, perhaps with attempts to discover a hiding place, but safety is now more important than a connection with the abusive family member.

Family involvement in the treatment of the survivor of elder abuse is a sensitive matter. It is of prime importance that the clinician ascertain for each family member any presence of collusion with the abuse, with the abusing behavior of the family member, or with the helplessness of the elderly survivor. Well-meaning therapeutic efforts can fail miserably and even cause further pain when a family member chosen for support opposes at some level the recovery of the survivor and the cessation of the abuse.

Treatment for the Abuser

Treatment of the abusing member of the family begins with the determination whether the abuse or neglect is primarily related to caregiving stress or to malevolent motives. To the degree that stress from providing elder care is the main problem, interventions may include the following:

- Individual, couple, or family counseling
- Support group for caregivers
- Education on caregiving, short- and long-term effects of mistreatment, and available programs
- Programs offering caregiver respite, such as help in the home, meals-on-wheels, respite workers
- Concrete and emotional support from friends, family, etc.

Interventions for malevolent mistreatment consist of the following:

- Individual counseling, drug and alcohol programs, inpatient or outpatient
- Educational groups modeled after those developed for younger batterers, to teach alternatives to violence
- Vocational counseling and placement
- Education on community resources and on the short- and long-term effects of mistreatment
- Police, court orders, and mandated programs; incarceration·
- Limited or cessation of contact with the victim
- Other living arrangements for abusers, e.g., nursing home, group home, separate apartment, house, or with friends or family (Breckman & Adelman, 1988, p. 64)

Family Treatment

Principal goals for the treatment of families having an abusive and/or abused elder member are threefold. First, whatever factors in the family system support the occurrence of abuse must be addressed and decreased. Next, family members must develop appropriate coping skills that do not lead to abuse. And finally the events that are precipitants to the abuse must be identified and eliminated. Using the elements listed above for the treatment of abusers and of survivors, the family therapist should construct an individualized treatment plan that reflects the particular situation of the family. In the treatment of elder abuse, the clinician should never use the intervention of prescribing the symptom or behavior, which in this instance would be the abusive behavior.

SUMMARY

This chapter has focused on some of the problems encountered by the elderly and their families, problems that are independent of the normal life cycle. Their pervasive significance for total family functioning, in addition to the frequency of their occurrence, combine to warrant their inclusion in this book. Thus we have addressed issues of family resistance to elders' independence, long-term care, depression and suicide, substance abuse, and elder abuse.

These issues do not stand alone. Their causes and patterns of expression are influenced greatly by societal factors. And societal factors are made manifest through administrative actions. It is therefore fitting to conclude the book with a chapter on policy and program planning.

Chapter 7

THE POLICY AND PROGRAM PLANNING BASE FOR FAMILY THERAPY WITH AGING PERSONS

MARILYN L. FLYNN

INTRODUCTION

This chapter reviews the connections between a systems-oriented, multigenerational approach to family therapy and the external policy environment within which these interventions must be delivered.

Social policies can powerfully reinforce or undermine the efforts of therapists to encourage redefinition of boundaries, hierarchies, and roles in a family. Administrative reorganization or changes in guidelines for health and welfare programs can precipitate crises and prevent families from reaching homeostasis. For example, insecurity that accompanies life cycle ltransitions such as retirement can be worsened by harsh tax laws or revisions in public and private pension requirements. Current policies in the United States tend to isolate younger families and children from the old and discourage intergenerational transfers of income or mutual assistance. On the other hand, trends may lend new support to family-centered treatment.

AGING, FAMILY POLICY, AND FAMILY THERAPY

Whatever their form, policies are intended to ensure consistent handling of comparable situations. Policies give practical expression to the mission and goals of an organization or a society. They set up the constraints within which programs are designed and implemented.

Policy appears in many guises—as rules, procedures, general guidelines for action, and broad goals statements. Policies may be formal and tangible, as in laws, regulations, manuals, or other documents. But they may also be informal and identifiable only through their behavioral consequences. For example, some organizations serving older clients have few members over 65 on their boards of directors. If the nominating committees were asked whether older persons were intentionally excluded from participation, the response would be indignant denial. Nonetheless private conversations might reveal a generally held belief that older board members are less alert and energetic and have difficulty following discussions. The result is unspoken agreement about board composition, which leaves governance in the hands of young community members. Informal policies—such as de facto segregation—may be more difficult to alter than formal policies. Much of the "ageism" that affects family life is a product of these de facto policy choices in the community.

Practitioners must be sensitive to public and private policies, whether formal or informal, that affect the success of interventions with elderly persons and their families. It might seem logical that the body of policy decisions most closely allied to these concerns would be "family policy." As it has evolved in other countries such as Sweden and France, family policy is indeed a consciously organized legislative agenda that is intended to impact the structure and functioning of families. Historically, family policy abroad has been almost entirely a response to issues of family fertility. While France, Sweden, and (the former) West Germany have unsuccessfully attempted to counter their declining birthrates, the People's Republic of China and India, among others, have sought to achieve the opposite effect and decrease fertility. In any event, no modern nation has interpreted family policy to include the aged as well as children. In fact, the elderly have been seen as competitors—for example, for housing and income support.

In the United States, no single piece of legislation at the federal level is widely acknowledged as policy to improve the social and economic well-being of all families. Family policy is confined to questions of child protection, child poverty, and child support under the Administration for Children and Families in the Department of Health and Human Services (HHS). Social legislation for aging persons is embodied in The Older Americans Act of 1965, implemented by the Administration on Aging in HHS. The Administration on Aging and the Administration for Children and Families have virtually no meaningful exchange with each other. Cash support for poor families under the Aid to Families with Dependent Children (AFDC) and the Supplemental Security Income (SSI) program for aged and disabled poor are housed in still another arm of HHS called the Assistance Payments Administration (APA). The APA is strictly occupied with transferring money for AFDC and SSI to states and considers itself entirely divorced from direct services.

Another unlikely arm of federal family policy is the Internal Revenue Service (IRS). The federal income tax system contains provisions that favor working low-income families, those with dependents and child-care needs, and certain other groups. However, the IRS hardly perceives itself as an instrument for protection of the multigenerational family unit.

In education, employment, and health care, the public policy stance is similar. Most benefits and services are oriented toward individuals or mothers and young children. Nowhere is consideration given to the full family unit, least of all to the potential interactions among older and younger generations. Within Congress, the Senate Special Committee on Aging periodically reviews policy from a broad perspective. It seeks to understand how older persons may be affected by contradictions, gaps, or other inadequacies in current legislation. The *family* is not, however, its particular concern.

Therefore in general it is correct to say that a multigenerational family systems approach receives little current support from the federal government as a matter of public policy. This by no means argues against the value of family interventions that engage both younger and older members. It explains in part, however, why practitioners may find it difficult to initiate or sustain this approach in a human service organization.

THE INTERACTION OF POLICY WITH SYSTEM BOUNDARIES, HIERARCHIES, AND ROLES IN FAMILIES

The importance of basing intervention with older persons on ecological perspectives has been a central theme of this book. The practitioner expects to intervene in a network of relationships as the context for problem solving. A central task is to expand the role repertoire of the family as it confronts changed life circumstances. Constructive adaptation may necessitate shifts in boundaries, hierarchies, or roles. Current public policies in the health and human service system may have important effects on these aspects of treatment.

System Boundaries

A family-centered, multigenerational approach clearly works best when the practitioner can freely bring any relevant member of the kinship group into treatment. Restrictions as to the legal nature of the relationships, geographic boundaries, age, or other criteria limit treatment options. When reimbursement for professional services is made through private insurance or public funds, the number of contacts with any particular family member—such as grandparent or child—ideally ought to be open to therapeutic discretion. The distinction between "collateral" and "client" contacts, so long familiar in many organizations, no longer should apply within the family group itself.

Furthermore some families may have important relationships with legally unrelated members who nonetheless occupy significant roles as parents, grandparents, or children. Other families may have members who are concurrently clients of one or more health and human service programs such as public assistance, adult foster care, and Medicaid. The setting for work with families must be open to flexible selection depending upon family composition and mobility. As suggested in previous chapters, a family therapist often may be more effective by providing home-based rather than clinic-based services. In instances where older persons are homebound, this approach might be particularly suitable. Policies should, under the best circumstances, encourage therapists to utilize the environment that best promotes understanding and resolution of family conflict.

Unfortunately American social policy has been highly segmented by age and problem categories. Funding is restricted and fosters fragmented and individualized service. The therapist may be working effectively to renegotiate interpersonal boundaries among family members. But the service system itself may create or reinforce other types of boundary problems. For example, in most community mental health clinics therapists' time can be reimbursed only for treatment of one identified patient, with a limit imposed on the number of "collateral" visits with relatives. Meetings must be clinic-based. If the older person is an identified client in another system—for example, Medicaid or public assistance—the type and duration of problems that can be addressed may be quite curtailed.

Boundary lines thus are defined not only by the psychodynamics of family life, but also by the health and human service system itself. Proponents of family therapy with the elderly will have to struggle against well-entrenched bureaucratic practices and procedures that reflect more general tendencies in the society toward infantilization and discounting of the aged. Examples include nursing home admissions policies that require family members to leave at intake because they will be "too disruptive," preretirement training programs that do not admit spouses, recreation programs that segregate children and older people, and publicly subsidized family housing facilities that define parents and children as a family unit but exclude grandparents.

Hierarchies

As noted in earlier chapters, the balance of status and power in families is subject to change throughout the life developmental cycle. This can be psychologically distressing for all generations involved. Unfortunately psychological resistance to these changes sometimes is reinforced by policies in the human service system.

One conspicuous example is the asset test in many states, which is applied to the aged, blind, and disabled applicants for public assistance programs. In order to conserve state funds, the principle of "relative responsibility" sometimes has been adopted. This requires that the resources of sons and daughters be considered in determining eligibility of the older persons for benefits. In effect it requires children to support their parents in case of need. If children refuse to accept this financial role, their parent is left in great distress. But agreeing to participate also means a reduced sense of independence for the older person, a forced realignment of family relationships, and often a reduced standard of welfare for the children.

Role Flexibility

Role flexibility has been described as an important correlate of successful aging and refers to the ability of families to respond effectively to challenges and unexpected upsets in daily living. Role flexibility means family members pitch in, carry different responsibilities, and harness strengths of older and younger members in creative ways.

It is in this area of role flexibility that social policy today perhaps militates most against adaptive multigenerational family problem solving. Since the founding of the Massachusetts Bay Colony in the 17th century, social policies in the United States have been "categorical" or selectively targeted to individuals with certain age or problem characteristics. The result is an array of cutoffs in program benefits that defies any holistic approach to family functioning or role adaptation.

A brief review of programs illustrates this point. Older widows of men who were the primary wage earners in the family may receive Survivor's Insurance under the Social Security Act. However, those women must have dependent children to be eligible. No funds are provided for skill training that would lead to economic independence. They are eligible for employment and training programs under the Older Americans Act if 55 or older, but only if income falls below federal poverty standards. Public housing might be available to these widows, depending on the ages of their children, but this option would close as soon as the youngest reaches 18 years of age. Women without children would be ineligible.

If dependent children in a widow's family were teenagers and interested in acquiring preemployment skills through public programs for the disadvantaged, these youth would be out of luck until age 16. Even then they would qualify for a full-year program only if they had dropped out of school.

In such families, the social system does little to support the traditional idea of parents and children working to make ends meet following loss of a pivotal member. An ingenious practitioner may be able to help the family assemble appropriate supports, but the framework of social legislation hardly promotes adaptive responses.

Cost containment has been a major focus of health-care policy since the 1970s. The chief policy instruments for controlling federal and state expenditures through Medicaid and Medicare programs have been co-pay requirements, deductibles, limits on length of health care service, restrictions on outpatient and home-based services, and limitations on prescription drugs. In addition most older people are unable to obtain glasses, hearing aids, or other needed specialized equipment. Those whose poverty or disability status makes them eligible for Medicaid may be better off, in this respect at least, than individuals living just above the state poverty standard or than members of the lower middle class. Routine screening and other programs that provide prevention or education services typically would not be covered, although public health departments sometimes make glaucoma testing or similar sight and hearing assessments available.

In addition to bearing the psychological and social trauma from loss of vision and hearing, older persons in poverty receive little material help with these problems from public programs. Private programs such as those funded by the United Way or local fraternal organizations (e.g., the Lions) can offer invaluable help. From the perspective of what might be available on a relatively uniform national basis, however, the picture is bleak.

GOODNESS OF FIT BETWEEN PUBLIC POLICY AND THE CHANGING FAMILY

Prior to 1965, there was little goodness-of-fit between the needs of aging families and American social policy. As average age increased and urbanization overtook rural life, retirement income for workers in the nation's cities became a pressing issue. In 1934, President Roosevelt demanded that Congress authorize social security legislation, drawing chiefly from the experience of prior German laws. The onset of old age was officially defined as age 65, and benefits under Old Age Insurance were strictly tied to previous contributions. A small assistance payment was authorized for destitute older people who did not qualify under the new system.

By the mid-1950s the growing proportion of older people in this country and improvements in the technology of health care were reflected in an unprecedented demand for hospital beds. Nearly a decade was spent on hospital construction, extension of the nursing care industry, and provision of benefits for acute care for patients without means to pay (Hill Burton Act of 1946). Passage of the Medicare and Medicaid amendments to the Social Security Act in 1965 (Title XVIII and XIX) entrenched a private, fee-for-service structure that to this day continues to foster hospital-based acute care.

In terms of "goodness-of-fit," the concept of the family embedded in the Social Security Act was a narrow one that had slowly been somewhat revised. Payments under the original retirement provisions of the Act were structured on the assumption that families would have a (male) breadwinner, full-time housewife, and few-to-no dependent children at the man's retirement. Since 1960 many unprecedented forms of family structure have attained wider foothold, including split and blended families, families with two parents permanently employed on a full-time basis, same-sex couples, single-parent households, never-married parents, and households of four or five generations. Both the social security system and the income tax system have struggled to come to terms with these developments. Equity considerations have clashed with fundamental divisions in the society about which forms of kinship relations should receive governmental sanction and support. Contemporary policies still favor the long-term worker, the long-term marriage, and the breadwinner with dependent spouse. Concessions have been introduced, however, that open eligibility to more divorced persons.

The trend in health-care programs is toward somewhat improved funding for home-based care in which all family members may participate. Major obstacles remain, however, in the credentialization of service providers as required by insurance companies and policies, which insist that the patient be hospitalized prior to initiation of home-based care. The effect of these restrictions is that families continue to be treated as "intruders." They cannot use techniques for mutual assistance that are permitted in advanced Western European countries and several developing nations. Relatives are forced to relate to their elder member as a patient. The United States health-care system reinforces dependence of families on outside professionals for routine care of older members to a greater extent than virtually anywhere else in the world.

Perhaps the most significant piece of legislation concerning the social needs of older persons in this country is the Older Americans Act of 1965. A direct result of the 1961 White House Conference on Aging, the Older Americans Act created the Administration on Aging in the Department of Health and Human Services (then HEW). Later amendments established a system of Area Agencies on Aging responsible for planning, funding, and coordinating services to all older persons.

Through passage of the Older Americans Act of 1965, the United States Congress has declared that all aging persons are entitled to "full and free enjoyment" of adequate income, community services, housing, employment opportunities, and "the best possible physical and mental health science can make available." To achieve these policy goals, the government authorized grants to states and communities for a full range of services designed to maintain independent living arrangements for older persons, reduce barriers to full participation in society, and establish a complete continuum of care for the frail and vulnerable older person.

The Older Americans Act was an emancipation proclamation for the elderly. Unlike most American social legislation, it was not categorical.

Programs funded under its provisions were—at least in theory—targeted at all older persons. Since 1982, amendments increasingly have stressed service to frail, vulnerable, disadvantaged, and minority populations. The original universal thrust of the Act has somewhat diminished. Nonetheless the vision still remains: Every older person should have access to a complete array of supportive services that protect, preserve, and enhance full membership in community life.

The Older Americans Act was focused initially on older people as individuals—their liberties, capacities, and rights in a democratic society. It was an offshoot of the civil rights and economic opportunity movement in philosophy and language, a frontal attack on ageism in the human services, labor market, and local civic institutions. Consequently the relationship of older persons to their families and the potential role of families in the provision of care was given comparatively little attention until recently.

NEW PRESSURES FOR FAMILY-FOCUSED POLICY IN ADDRESSING NEEDS OF OLDER PERSONS

Since 1983, the federal government has been shifting toward greater emphasis on family responsibility in several legislative arenas, including the Older Americans Act. Family respite care of ill older persons, subsidies for adult caretakers who devote substantial proportions of their time to care of older dependent relatives, and family-oriented services to victims of Alzheimer's disease are examples. Experimentation with recreated or substitute family environments in congregate living arrangements have long been an interest of architects and those working on housing needs of the elderly.

A second trend favoring a family systems approach to working with older people is accelerating pressure at both the state and federal levels for coordinated, family-oriented services. Certainly in the case of high-risk children and adults, a fragmented, sequential approach to service provision produces unsatisfactory outcomes with high long-term cost to the community. Area Agencies on Aging have experimented for several years with specialized case coordination units in order to maximize benefits of existing services. Experience is gradually cumulating that should allow public and private agencies alike to implement multi-sector, family-focused services better than at any previous period since World War II.

It should be noted, however, that family-focused interventions have consistently been undermined by many factors. Examples include lack of worker orientation to the family system, funding that can be expended only for certain age or problem categories, interdisciplinary rivalry among professionals about how problems should be defined or treated, and inadequate resources. Perhaps most challenging is the clinical issue of how to establish plans and goals for family members where needs for assistance may range among individuals from intensive interventions such as detoxification to preventive programs or career guidance. When practitioners try to mix sectors (e.g., health, mental health, education) and levels of care (institutional, outpatient) among different persons in the same family unit, all the worst obstacles in the fragmented human services system surface.

OLD AGAINST YOUNG IN PURSUIT OF SERVICES: CAN A FAMILY SYSTEMS PERSPECTIVE HELP?

As the child poverty rate rose steadily during the 1980s, there was a surge in complaints that the aging population was receiving "too much" or more than its "fair share" of social goods relative to younger families and children. This claim has been supported by the analysis of trends in government spending and social well-being since 1960. Supporters of this view argued that people over 65 had gained more from federal programs than any other age group. And it is now true that over one fifth of total federal expenditures for all purposes and 45% of all federal outlays for social welfare are allocated for the aged. Fully half the nation's elderly are lifted from poverty by these federal programs. This exceeds the estimated federal social welfare expenditures for any other age group.

Further, studies of the redistributional effects of social security payments show that each cohort of workers since 1935 so far has received more in retirement benefits than it contributed in social security taxes. Looking ahead, there will be fewer workers between 1990 and 2010 to support a larger number of retired persons living into their 80s and 90s. With persistent lackluster improvements in productivity of the United Stated economy, younger families will need to finance the social security system out of higher taxes and possibly a reduced standard of living. The intergenerational transfer from young to old will thus be increased even more.

The share of national income allocated to older people has also been challenged by other groups who have learned since the 1960s how to exercise power and prominence for public attention. Women, representatives of ethnic and racial minorities, AIDS victims, environmentalists, and others with valid social claims have struggled for congressional influence. Thus the pattern continues of contending old against young, old against other victims of discrimination, and old against those with similar problems of disease or poverty.

Pitting young against old in public policy debate repeats a tendency noted above to view older people as a separate category, competing for scarce resources with other groups in society. For those who believe that social gains can best be achieved through a clash of powerful political interest groups, the competition of lobbyists for older people with child advocates seems inevitable.

Practitioners with a multigenerational, family systems approach to problem solving have a significant contribution to make in this contentious policy arena. As argued in previous chapters, intergenerational issues are often triggered by the transition from one stage of the life cycle to another. Critical junctures in people's lives also occur as a result of accidents, family disruption through divorce, onset of long-term disease, or changes in general economic conditions. These experiences of adversity occur among young and old alike. Common needs result.

For example, modified public transportation for the disabled is a generalized requirement of most persons, irrespective of age, who are confined to a wheelchair. Yet public authorities have resisted pooling vans or cars from different agencies when the client populations vary in age. Public housing funds have been allocated to "family" sites as opposed to sites for older persons, with political lobbying pushing for the distribution of resources between the two groups. Nursing homes have been perceived as being centers for the care of the elderly, with few public funds outside of Medicaid for support of the young who need shelter care or longer-term intermediate nursing and physical rehabilitation. Home-delivered services such as nursing, meals, and domestic assistance have been relatively undeveloped for children and young adults until recently, though supported under the Older Americans Act for those over 60.

Blending the uses of resources means more intergenerational contact and mediation of differences. It means challenging widely shared beliefs among all generations about the nature of youth, adulthood, and aging. In particular, it means that helping professionals would need to respond to an altered array of problems arising from service utilization. Older people may be disturbed by children's noise in a van. Insurers may raise questions. Some caregivers may feel comfortable with dependent younger adults but not the aged. From a family systems perspective, however, many of these problems will be familiar and remediable. Resource sharing is unlikely to be accepted on a large scale basis without the understanding and techniques that are integral to intervention with family systems.

SPECIAL POLICY ISSUES IN FAMILIES WITH AGING MEMBERS: WORK, INCOME, AND RETIREMENT

Poverty Policy and Older Persons

In 1935, the Social Security Act stated that adequate income for older persons was a national goal. This aim was again reasserted in the Older Americans Act. Between 1965 and 1990, the poverty rate among persons age 65 or over was reduced by nearly two-thirds, from 33% to 12.4%. This has been accomplished through a complex array of public policy provisions including social insurance, public assistance, food stamps, subsidized housing, medical insurance (Medicare), medical assistance (Medicaid), and special tax relief measures. To some it seems as if older Americans enjoy an elaborate, well-financed system of protections against poverty, ill health, and economic insecurity. However, these figures are deceptive. Whites are less likely than African-Americans, Native Americans, and some other minorities to be poor in older age. Because of shorter life expectancies among racial minorities in this country, whites constitute 90% of those over 65—a larger proportion than among other age groups. If African-Americans are compared, poverty rates for young and old are equal—31% in both cases, and the rate has increased by 22% since 1978 after falling in the previous two decades.

Aged persons of all races are far more likely than younger families or individuals to have incomes just above the poverty line. Two out of every five older people have income just above subsistence; that is, under 200% of the federal poverty line. A potentially disturbing trend for the future is the status of the Supplemental Security Income (SSI). This program is targeted at the elderly and disabled poor. Benefits are tied to the Consumer Price Index and also were increased in 1984 and 1985. So many cuts were made in other programs on which SSI recipients depend, however—such as Food Stamps and Medicaid—that some older people actually fell deeper into poverty even while receiving SSI.

The view that elderly persons are well off is also unfortunate from a family systems perspective. Although benefits within many human service programs have improved in real terms, little attention has been given to the *interaction* of eligibility requirements *between programs*. When assistance, insurance, in-kind benefits, and other services are considered as a package, the net effect on older people is to discourage labor force participation, shared living arrangements, and transfer of income between younger and older generations. These are all consequences with special meaning to those interested in family systems and the preservation of multigenerational relationships.

Furthermore despite the improvements in well-being of older people, aged women—both poor and nonpoor—remain at an economic disadvantage to men. Whether divorced, widowed, separated, or never married, a greater percentage of women over 65 have inadequate or below subsistence income. Widows of workers eligible for private pensions often receive no survivor's benefits, and social security benefits drop by one third when the husband dies (assuming the wife has not achieved her own pension eligibility). In addition, because women have histories of lower earning and less continuity in their work history, they are likely to receive lower social security and private pension benefits even if drawing on their own records. Finally women elect early retirement more often than men. This decision carries with it a permanent reduction in benefits—about 20% in the case of social security should retirement begin at age 62. While public assistance payments under Supplemental Security Income can ameliorate the worst effects for women with very small pension incomes, the remainder live in continuous economic insecurity.

CHANGING CONCEPTS OF RETIREMENT, POLICY CONFLICTS, AND THE CONTRIBUTION OF A FAMILY SYSTEMS PERSPECTIVE

No single definition of retirement has ever satisfied all groups concerned with this concept. Changes occur often over many years in the amount of work, level of earnings, eligibility for pension benefits, career commitment, self-concept, and social status of an aging individual. The notion of retirement itself is an invention of urbanized Western societies. It assumed widespread meaning in this country only after World War II.

Three principal factors contributed to this development. First, improved health care and the elimination of many fatal childhood diseases meant that a larger proportion of the general population survived to age 70 or beyond. Second, there was strong impetus for removing older people from the workplace both during the depression and in 1945 as a method of job creation for younger workers and later, returning veterans. Finally the rapid pace of a manufacturing economy demanded that employees perceived to be less efficient step aside so that competitive levels of output could be maintained. Older people were often considered to be less productive.

The practice of fixed-age retirement at age 65 as settled upon in most public and private pension systems was another comparatively new idea. It represents a sharp departure from traditional work patterns in a more rural economy. Older people in farm communities used to remain involved in some aspects of production as long as they chose and were physically able. Reduction of activity was gradual, not abrupt. Fixed-age "retirement" as commonly understood today can thus be seen as an artifact of industrial economic life. It has not evolved as an expression of aging people's own psychological, physiological, or family needs. Few should be surprised that this bureaucratically defined event should present so many hurdles for families to surmount.

From the vantage point of public policy and the administration of pension benefits, withdrawal from participation in the labor force has traditionally constituted the primary "test" of retirement, together with age. Therefore older people who have reentered the labor market after applying for pension benefits suffer penalties of earnings. Over a relatively low limit, they lose one dollar of pension benefits for every two dollars of earnings, or a 50% "tax" on work effort. Some workers are disinclined to remain in the labor force and others limit their part-time work in order not to exceed the maximum. People with low or modest pension benefits who need to supplement their retirement benefits are harmed most by this provision.

Social security pension benefits are calculated on the basis of average earnings for a minimum period of 10 years. Earnings periods need not be continuous, but people generally boost their earnings average most toward the end of their careers, when wages or salaries are often highest. Unfortunately some workers are driven out of the labor force in middle age due to poor health, job discrimination, plant closings, recession, or economic restructuring. The Northeast and Midwest have comparatively large pools of older people who have been exposed to job loss for these reasons at peak periods in their careers. A disproportionate number are minority group members. Most will have no private pension benefits, are unwilling to retire, but have no options except to enroll in the social security program at the earliest possible retirement age of 62. They will be left with reduced lifetime benefits and few means to supplement their income. These individuals can also be expected to experience dissatisfaction with retirement as well as face economic disadvantage.

Governments historically have used retirement policy as a tool for stabilizing the economy and preventing social unrest. The underlying assumption in a fixed-age retirement model is that older people will disengage from society, reduce their activity level, and decline with each advancing year. This traditional view also emphasizes the necessity of *compulsory* rather than voluntary retirement, with the expectation of complete withdrawal by the individual from employment. Leisure is seen as something distinct from work. This framework supports policy objectives of job creation with an ideology that perpetuates some of the worst elements of ageism.

An alternative policy perspective on retirement has gained legislative attention to some extent since the 1961 White House Conference on Aging. Proponents maintain that retirement should present opportunities for activity and sustained work and for integration of work with leisure. Withdrawal from work should not be sudden or climactic but, in keeping with individual wishes, it ought to be phased or gradual. Timing in terms of age should be flexible and reversible. Older people should be freed of stereotypical thinking about their abilities and capacities as they age. They should consider themselves instead in light of their potentialities and strengths.

Partly in response to these views, "early" and "delayed" retirement provisions have been added to most public pensions, and penalties for labor force participation have been slightly modified. Compulsory retirement in the majority of occupations has been eliminated under the Age Discrimination Act. Job sharing, flex time, and growth in permanent part-time work opportunities have expanded the mechanisms for labor force participation by older persons. The federal government has created a few programs that attempt to widen employment or volunteer options for the elderly.

On the other hand the absence of employment, retraining, and vocational rehabilitation programs for older persons has serious implications for retirement and late-life adjustment. Middle-aged persons who suffer poor health or mild-to-moderate disabilities are particularly disposed to opt for early retirement with reduced pension benefits. They typically are unlikely to have private pension benefits. Disproportionate numbers are members of racial minorities. European countries have long established many methods for helping people who experience employment difficulties in late middle age. The United States has been extremely slow to respond.

Family life is deeply affected by the gaps and traditionalistic orientation of the American public pension system. High-income families who can combine private and public pensions with voluntary timing of retirement will meet the challenge best. Others will experience unnecessarily heightened problems of psychological and social adjustment.

HEALTH, INDEPENDENCE, AND LONG-TERM CARE

At any one time, only about 5% of the persons age 65 or over are residents of nursing homes. During the course of a 12-month period, however, over 20% of this population has one or more stays in a long-term care facility. It has long been assumed that the primary reason for placement is ill health. Recent studies have shown, however, that the major determinant of placements directly from home to nursing care facilities is *change in health or welfare of other family members*.

For example, incontinence is not of itself a serious medical problem. Yet it is one of the primary reasons given by relatives for referral to long-term care institutions. When does incontinence become insupportable? Perhaps divorce or other stressful life events prevent a caretaker from being present as regularly. The wife may no longer be able to support the weight of a disabled spouse in moving him from bed to bathroom. A new dependent member may join the household. These and other upheavals mean that families cannot pool their energies or focus their attention on the elder member as effectively. Nursing home care seems inevitable.

This illustration highlights the vital point that nursing home or residential care is often more a response to *social* and *interpersonal* factors than medical conditions alone. Maintaining independent living arrangements of older people is therefore a complex interaction between adequate supportive services, service access, service coordination, and *family involvement*. The service array must be organized in light of needs felt by all relevant members of the family unit, including children or other relatives who have direct responsibilities for care of aging relatives.

Home-based care has been advocated as a lower-cost alternative to institutionalization. Some recent data suggest, however, that there may be little real difference between home-based and facility-based costs of care. The justification must lie more in the value systems of professionals and families with elder members. The pernicious effects of long-term residential care for some adults have often been noted: isolation from community, decreased intellectual functioning, decline in physical well-being, diminished interpersonal competence, and attenuation of family ties. To the extent that social policy encourages the ideal of meaningful incorporation of aging persons in community life, home-based and coordinated care must be expanded.

LOOKING TO THE FUTURE: AGING, PUBLIC POLICY, AND FAMILY SYSTEMS INTERVENTION

Several trends are likely to affect public policy for the aged and their families during the 1990s. As the proportion of very aged and frail individuals over 80 increases, demands on funds under the Older Americans Act will grow even more fierce. It is possible that federal and state resources will be reallocated away from individuals and families under 70. New definitions of who is "old" may emerge, and as a result, new expectations will be brought to bear on "young" individuals in their 60s. In short, society may reevaluate the anticipated periods for length of labor force participation, family care, and self-care.

Computer and communications technology have slowly been revolutionizing the home. Toasters, refrigerators, telephones, automobiles, calculators, furnaces, lights, and most of the equipment in everyday life contain the ubiquitous memory chip. Computer and communications linkages make possible the monitoring of older persons in their homes, the purchase of food and other services for home delivery, new forms of home-based, part-time work, specialized aids to increase mobility of the severely disabled, and even the administration of medication. For the middle- and upper-income retirees, home will never have been a more hospitable place nor the world more readily within reach. As video features are more embedded in communications equipment, it will be possible for therapists to arrange family conferences by telephone in which all members can see and hear one another. Conferencing by electronic mail will also represent another alternative for families with several working members who cannot be present at the same time. These and other innovative applications of technology will give family therapists greater scope for intervention. Some of the barriers to family interaction such as distance or physical frailty can now only be addressed through transportation or other demand-responsive, costly services. With electronic linkages, the insufficiency of current services may be circumvented even when individuals are physically distant or immobile.

For the poor, however, the prospects are ominous. If no changes are made in public assistance or health insurance legislation, the living standard of older persons now in poverty will continue to drop. While rates of poverty may not rise, the degree of impoverishment among those already poor will. The amount of coordinated resources needed to bring these unfortunate elders back to living at or above subsistence level will also be greater. Targeting and earmarking of funds by Congress to alleviate favored problems or special groups is also likely to mount. Pressures on families to provide care for their own members will heighten. The task of systems-oriented practitioners in addressing the problems of this group will be even more formidable.

Coverage of different age groups and disease entities under social health insurance is expanding incrementally, much as old age insurance was painstakingly extended over the years. Catastrophic illness, some forms of long-term care, Alzheimer's disease, and prescription drugs may be brought under the social security umbrella. Not all older people and their families will benefit equally. The redistributional effects will depend on which income levels bear the greatest burden of inevitable tax increases. The degree of economic insecurity for everyone will be reduced, however, when the specter of uncontrollable medical expenses is less haunting.

State and federal governmental restraints on health and welfare spending may persist until the 21st century. This will drive policymakers to emphasize reallocation or redirection of existing resources. Family-oriented approaches to treatment have already received fresh attention and are likely to attract renewed endorsement. To the extent that therapists can demonstrate an ability to reach across multiple sectors to combine resources, they will also capitalize on deepening public support for coordinated service strategies.

The forces that freed societal perspectives of the elderly from traditional myths gave a new place to older persons as individuals. The next step to be taken in the last decade of the 20th century is to reconceptualize empowered older persons in their appropriate and necessary relationships to other family members. The family systems approach provides a set of values, organizing principles, and methods for achieving this goal.

APPENDIX A:
Outline for Family Assessment

I. Identifying Information
   A. Family members in household. Names, relationships, birth dates, marriage dates, education, occupations, employers, income.
   B. Significant others in or outside household. Names, ages, relationships, current locations.

II. Presenting Problems/Needs/Requests
   A. Reason for application.
      1. Who initiated contact and how?
      2. Who recognized problems/needs?
      3. When was problem/need recognized?
      4. Date of initial contact.
   B. Nature of problems/needs/requests.
      1. Description (what and about whom).
      2. Precipitating factors.
      3. Onset and pervasiveness.
      4. Different/similar perceptions and reactions of family members.
   C. Effect of problems/needs/requests on family.
      1. How is this situation a problem for each person?
      2. How does each person explain the problem or need?
      3. How is the family different as a result of the problem event?
      4. What implications does the problem/need have for the future of the family?
   D. Meaning of helping by family and outsiders.
      1. What is the family belief system about seeking help from outside the family?

2. How were the problems/needs of the elderly handled in the past?
3. What are the helping patterns about elderly family members in this generation?
4. What has the family done so far to resolve the current problems/needs presented?
5. What are the positive and negative consequences of the family helping effort?
6. What are the individual concerns about involvement in future helping?

E. Expectations about change.
1. What do family members believe should be done next?
2. What do family members believe is necessary from helpers outside the family?
3. What changes does each person desire most?
4. What are the problem-solving ideas of family members?
5. Who outside the family system should be involved in the therapeutic system?

III. Family System
A. Structure and boundaries.
1. What are the formal roles in this family (for father, mother, grandparent, etc.)?
2. What are the informal roles in this family (for caretakers, mediators, healers, historian)?
3. How satisfied are individuals with their roles? Who feels stressed or overloaded?
4. How have roles changed in recent years, particularly those of older adults? Do people find the family flexible when needed?
5. Do individuals feel that others are available for support when needed? Are people reliable?
6. What are the major triangles and alliances? How are these helping or hindering the family at this stage?
7. Are there cutoffs among family members? If so, what are the effects?
8. Who holds power in the family? How is this expressed? How does this affect decisions that need to be made at this time?
9. Is there a sense of loyalty in the family?
10. How do members believe their relationships need to be changed to meet the current problems/needs of the family?
11. How does the practitioner describe family boundaries and the need for renegotiation in relation to resolving the problem?

B. Communication.
1. What are the major channels of communication in the family? Who speaks to whom and about what?
2. What are the taboos? What is not mentioned?

3. What is the family style of communication both verbally and non-verbally?
4. How do members believe communication has changed over the years?
5. Do family members feel free to express thoughts and feelings openly? When do they feel constrained?
6. How are anger, caring, and humor expressed and tolerated?
7. What do older adults worry about in communicating with younger members?
8. What changes would people like? What would be the consequences of such changes?
9. How would the practitioner describe the family in terms of clarity and ambiguity? What changes are needed?

C. Family through time. (Use genogram.)
1. How are current stages of individuals and the family as a whole related to problems/needs?
2. What significant history about the current family helps or hinders problem resolution?
3. What links do family members see between the current problem and patterns from the past?
4. What intergenerational patterns about aging are significant in the current situation?
5. What do family members value most from their intergenerational legacy (traditions, myths, stories, values, etc.)?
6. Are there significant cutoffs that affect the current situation?
7. Are there relationships and resources that could be activated to help in the current problem?

D. Transactions with larger systems. (Use ecomap.)
1. Is the family open to contact with larger systems? What is the family style?
2. How does the family describe its relationship with the outside world?
3. What are the sources of strain and support with other systems?
4. What supports and resources are currently being used?
5. What supports and resources need to be found or activated?
6. How has the family changed over time in its relationship with the outside world?

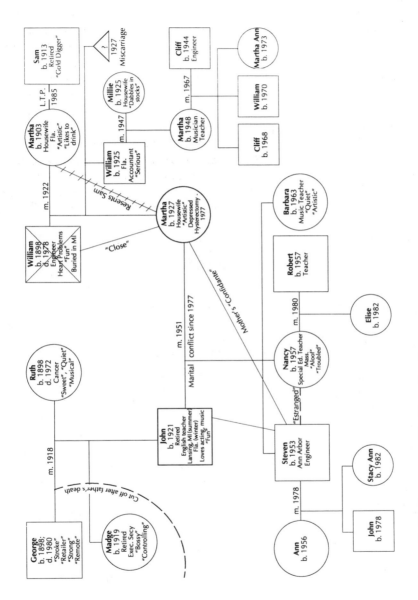

Appendix B. Genogram — The Berry Family

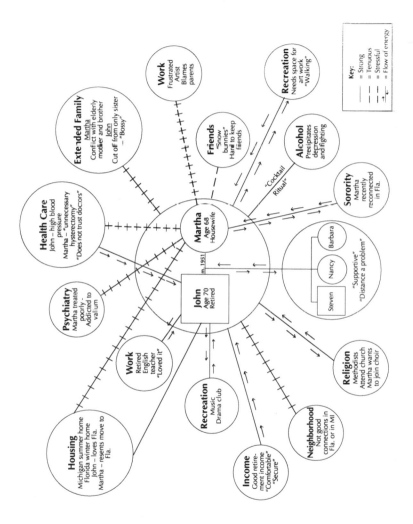

Appendix C. Ecomap —The Berry Family

Appendix D

Cultural Value Preferences of Middle-Class White Americans and Ethnic Minorities:
A Comparative Summary

Area of Relationships	Middle-Class White Americans	Asian/Pacific Americans	American Indian Alaskan Native	Black Americans	Hispanic Americans
Man to nature/ environment	Mastery over	Harmony with	Harmony with	Harmony with	Harmony with
Time orientation	Future	Past-present	Present	Present	Past-present
Relations with people	Individual	Collateral	Collateral	Collateral	Collateral
Preferred mode of activity	Doing	Doing	Being-in-becoming	Doing	Being-in-becoming
Nature of good and bad man	Good and bad	Good	Good	Good and bad	Good

SOURCE: Taken from Ho, M. K. *Family Therapy with Ethnic Minorities*. (1987). Reprinted by permission.

APPENDIX E:
Guidelines for the Prevention of Elder Abuse

For the Individual:

Stay sociable as you age; maintain and increase your network of friends and acquaintances.

Keep in contact with old friends and neighbors if you move in with a relative or change to a new address.

Develop a "buddy" system with a friend outside the home. Plan for at least a weekly contact and share openly with this person.

Ask friends to visit you at home; even a brief visit can allow observations of your well-being.

Accept new opportunities for activities. They can bring new friends.

Participate in community activities as long as you are able.

Volunteer or become a member or officer of an organization. Participate regularly.

Have your own telephone; post and open your own mail. If your mail is being intercepted, discuss the problem with the postal authorities.

Stay organized. Keep your belongings neat and orderly. Make sure others are aware that you know where everything is kept.

Take care of your personal needs. Keep regular medical, dental, barber, hairdresser, and other personal appointments.

Arrange to have your Social Security or pension check deposited directly to a bank account.

Get legal advice about arrangements you can make now for possible future disability, including powers of attorney, guardianships, or conservatorships.

Keep records, accounts, and property available for examination by someone you trust, as well as by the person you or the court has designated to manage your affairs.

Review your will periodically.

Give up control of your property or assets only when *you* decide you cannot manage them.

Ask for help when you need it. Discuss your plans with your attorney, physician, or family members.

Don't live with a person who has a background of violent behavior or alcohol or drug abuse.

Don't leave your home unattended. Notify police if you are going to be away for a long period. Don't leave messages on the door while you are away.

Don't leave cash, jewelry, or prized possessions lying about.

Don't accept personal care in return for transfer or assignments of your property or assets unless a lawyer, advocate, or another trusted person acts as a witness to the transaction.

Don't sign a document unless someone you trust has reviewed it.

Don't allow anyone else to keep details of your finances or property management from you.

For the Family:

Maintain close ties with aging relatives and friends. Keep abreast of changes in their health and ability to live independently.

Discuss an older relative's wishes regarding health care, terminal medical care alternatives, home care in the case of incapacitation, and disposition of his/her personal assets.

Find sources of help and *use* them. Chore services, housekeeping, home-delivered meals, senior recreation, day care, respite care, and transportation assistance are available in many communities.

With the older person's consent, become familiar with his/her financial records, bank accounts, will, safe deposit boxes, insurance, debts, and sources of income before he/she becomes incapacitated. Talk and plan together *now* about how these affairs should be handled.

Anticipate potential incapacitation by planning as a family who will take responsibility such as power-of-attorney or in-home caregiving if an aging relative becomes incapacitated.

Closely examine your family's ability to provide long-term, in-home care for a frail and increasingly dependent relative. Consider the family's physical limits.

Plan how your own needs will be met when your responsibility for the dependent older relative increases.

Explore alternative sources of care, including nursing homes or other relatives' homes, in case your situation changes.

Discuss your plans with friends, neighbors, and other sources of support before your responsibilities become a burden. Ask for their understanding and emotional support—you may need them.

Familiarize family members with emergency response agencies and services available in case of sudden need.

Don't offer personal home care unless you thoroughly understand and can meet the responsibilities and costs involved.

Don't wait until a frail older person has moved in with you to examine his/her needs. You'll need to consider access, safety, containment, and special needs. (Do you need a first-floor bathroom, bedroom, or entry ramp? Will carpets or stairs become barriers? Do you need a fenced yard to prevent the loved one from wandering away? Does your kitchen allow you to prepare special diets or store medications properly? Can you move the person safely in case of fire?)

Don't assume that poor interpersonal relationships between you, or other members of the household, and the older person involved will disappear.

Don't expect irritating habits or problems such as alcohol abuse to stop or be controlled once the dependent moves into your home.

Don't ignore your limitations and over-extend yourself. Passive neglect could result.

Don't hamper the older person's independence or intrude unnecessarily upon his/her privacy. Provide a private telephone if you can and make other changes if possible.

Don't label your efforts a failure if home care is not possible and you must seek an alternative.

SOURCE: Taken from Douglass, Richard L. *Domestic Mistreatment of the Elderly: Towards Prevention.* © 1987, American Association of Retired Persons. Reprinted with permission.

GLOSSARY

Ageism. Prejudices and stereotypes applied to older people based solely on their age.

Boundary. The part of a system that distinguishes what is within the system from what is outside it.

Channels of communication. Means by which people communicate with one another that are either visual, auditory, or kinesthetic (involving touch). See Bandler and Grinder (1976).

Circular questioning. An intervention by which family members are systemically investigated during a family session, with each member in turn being asked his/her view of a specific aspect of the family functioning. Usually a direct intervention for first order change, but can be used as an indirect intervention. See Selvini Palazzoli, Boscolo, Cecchin, and Prata (1980); Cecchin (1987).

Constructivism. The theory that reality is not discovered but is invented. One's reality is constrained by one's perceptions and experiences.

Direct intervention. An intervention aimed at first-order change. Involves the therapist sharing clinical expertise with the client(s). Evokes a response of compliance from family members.

Disengagement. In systems and their boundaries, the quality of family members' lack of connection with each other, their alienation from one another. Opposite pole of enmeshment.

Ecology. The science concerned with the interrelationship of organisms and their environment.

Ecomap. A diagram of the family and its relationship with external resources. A tool for assessment.

Eco-system. The complex of a human system, in this text a family and its environment, which function together as a unit in nature.

Enmeshment. In systems and their boundaries, the quality of family members' overinvolvement with each other. Opposite of disengagement.

First-order change. A change within the family that does not change the intrinsic nature of the family system. See Watzlawick, Weakland, and Fisch (1974).

Genogram. An intergenerational map of three or more generations of a family. A tool for assessment.

Goodness-of-fit. The need for individuals and principal groups to be in a supportive relationship with their physical and social environments and with the political and economic structures of society. See Germain and Gitterman (1980).

Joining. The means by which the clinician conveys to the family members that they are understood and that the clinician is working with and for the family. Both an attitude and a therapeutic technique for engaging the family in the therapeutic process.

Hierarchy. The organization of a family's several generations, each holding a different level of status and power.

Homeostasis. A feature of systems theory stating that the behavior of one family member is felt and responded to by other members in such a way that the system maintains itself without change.

Hypothesizing. The act of making a therapeutic formulation. As an element related to the intervention of circular questioning, is the starting point for investigation.

Indirect intervention. An intervention aimed at second-order change and achieved by implied or conflicting messages with differing amounts of clarity and directness. Clients may be unaware of the message. Examples: positive connotation and reframing the behavior or situation, restraining change, re-storying, assignments of a ritual.

Life review. An organized inventory of one's life, more than a simple recall of the past. A direct intervention.

Linear view of therapeutic change. The view of change that perceives clinical processes to be in terms of cause and effect.

Neutrality. Refers to the effect of the clinician's behavior on the family. A concept related to the intervention of circular questioning. Provides the reference for building hypotheses.

Positive connotation or labeling. A form of reframing by which a negative behavior is given a positive meaning. A form of indirect intervention.

Prescribing a ritual or ordeal. An indirect intervention by which the clinician instructs the family member(s) to do more of a problematic behavior, even to make it into an ordeal.

Reframing. (a) Restating the problem, issue, situation, behavior in different terms than were presented by the clients, resulting in a new view of the problem; (b) a type of indirect intervention that gives a particular situation or behavior a different meaning as a method of effecting change.

Reminiscence. A remembering of the past, used as an intervention with older adults.

Re-storying. The telling and restating of a family's or individual's story, with relevant meanings. An indirect intervention.

Restraining the symptom or change. An indirect intervention in which the family is instructed not to change a problematic behavior, or even not to change at all.

Ritual. A pattern of social interaction that is organized, repeated, predictable, bearing a social message or meaning. Examples: holiday dinners, patterns of greeting, family members' positions at the dinner table, spouses' predinner cocktail.

Role flexibility. The presence of a variety of responses that are adaptive to the situation and that permit family members to share and reassign tasks and responses to developmental needs and crises related to aging.

Sandwich generation. The generation of middle-aged adults, often in four- and five-generation families, whose parents/grandparents increasingly require attention and whose children have returned home for financial and emotional aid, perhaps bringing their own little children with them. A generation vulnerable to experiencing extreme stress.

Second-order change. A change within the family that changes the basic nature of the family system. See Watzlawick, Weakland, and Fisch (1974).

System. In this book the cybernetic definition is used. Not a social organization; instead, a unit containing feedback structure and therefore competent to process information.

Triangulation. A pulling of a vulnerable third person into the social interaction between two others who have become anxious in that interaction. May become fixed, permanent, and important in intergenerational systems, being repeated in subsequent generations.

REFERENCES

Antonucci, T., & Akiyama, H. (1991). Social relationships and aging well. *Generations, 15,* 39-44.

Bandler, R., & Grinder, J. (1975). *The structure of magic* (Vol. 1). Palo Alto, CA: Science & Behavior Books.

Bandler, R., & Grinder, J. (1976). *The structure of magic* (Vol. 2). Palo Alto, CA: Science & Behavior Books.

Bateson, G. (1971). A systems approach. *International Journal of Psychiatry, 9,* 242-244.

Blazer, D. (1991). Spirituality and aging well. *Generations, 15* (1), 61-65.

Bowen, M. (1978). *Family therapy in clinical practice.* New York: Jason Aronson.

Boyd-Franklin, N. (1989). *Black families in therapy: A multisystems approach.* New York: Guilford.

Breckman, R. S., & Adelman, R. D. (1988). *Strategies for helping victims of elder mistreatment.* Newbury Park, CA: Sage.

Butler, R. N., & Lewis, M. I. (1982). *Aging and mental health* (3rd ed.). St. Louis, MO: C. V. Mosby.

Carter, E., & McGoldrick, M. (Eds.). (1980). *The family life cycle: A framework for family therapy.* New York: Gardner.

Cecchin, G. (1987). Hypothesizing, circularity, and neutrality revisited. *Family Process, 26,* 405-413.

Douglass, R. L. (1987). *Domestic mistreatment of the elderly — Towards prevention.* Washington, DC: American Association of Retired Persons.

Duffy, M., Iscoe, I., & Kurman, R. G. (1982, October). *Geriatric crises in the family.* Panel presentation at the 40th Annual Conference, American Association of Marriage and Family Therapy, Dallas, TX.

Erikson, E. (1950). *Childhood and society.* New York: Norton.

Feinauer, L., Lund, D., & Miller, J. (1987). Family issues in multigenerational households. *American Journal of Family Therapy, 15*(7), 52-61.

Fleuridas, C., Nelson, T. S., & Rosenthal, D. M. (1986). The evolution of circular questions: Training family therapists. *Journal of Marital and Family Therapy, 12*, 113-127.

Friedman, E. H. (1980). Systems and ceremonies: A family view of rites of passage. In E. Carter & M. McGoldrick (Eds.), *The family life cycle: A framework for family therapy* (pp. 429-460). New York: Gardner.

Furman, B., & Ahola, T. (1988). Return of the question "why": Advantages of exploring pre-existing explanations. *Family Process, 27*, 395-409.

Garrison, J. E., Jr. (1989). Sexual dysfunction in the elderly: Causes and effects. In G. A. Hughston, V. A. Christopherson, & M. J. Bonjean (Eds.), *Aging and family therapy: Practitioner perspectives on Golden Pond* (pp. 149-162). New York: Haworth.

Germain, C., & Gitterman, A. (1980). *The life model of social work practice.* New York: Columbia University Press.

Goldberg, G. S., Kantrow, R., Kremen, E., & Lauter, L. (1986). Spouseless, childless elderly women and their social supports. *Social Work, 31*, 104-112.

Haley, J. (1976). *Problem-solving therapy.* New York: Harper & Row.

Haley, J. (1980). *Leaving home.* New York: McGraw-Hill.

Hartman, A. (1978, October). Diagrammatic assessment of family relationships. *Social Casework, 59*, 465-476.

Hartman, A., & Laird, J. (1983). *Family-centered social work practice.* New York: Free Press.

Haugland, S. (1989). Alcoholism and other drug dependencies in the aging patient. *Primary Care, 16*(2), 411-429.

Herr, J. J., & Weakland, J. H. (1979). *Counseling elders and their families: Practical techniques for applied gerontology.* New York: Springer.

Herz, F. (1980). The impact of death and serious illness on the family life cycle. In E. Carter & M. McGoldrick (Eds.), *The family life cycle: A framework for family therapy* (pp. 223-240). New York: Gardner.

Ho, M. K. (1987). *Family therapy with ethnic minorities.* Newbury Park, CA: Sage.

Hoffman, L. (1981). *Foundations of family therapy.* New York: Basic Books.

Hoffman, L. (1983). A co-evolutionary framework for systemic family therapy. In J. C. Hansen & B. P. Keeney (Eds.), *Diagnosis and assessment in family therapy* (pp. 35-61). Rockville, MD: Aspen.

Hoffman, L. (1985). Beyond power and control: Toward a "second order" family systems therapy. *Family Systems Medicine, 3*, 381-396.

Huber, J. R. (1985, October). *Assessment and intervention with older adults.* Paper presented at the Pre-Conference Institute on Creative Aging, American Association of Marriage and Family Therapy, New York.

Hughston, G. A., Christopherson, V. A., & Bonjean, M. J. (Eds.). (1989). *Aging and family therapy: Practitioner perspectives on Golden Pond.* New York: Haworth.

Hughston, G. A., & Cooledge, N. J. (1989). The life review: An underutilized strategy for systemic family intervention. In G. A. Hughston, V. A. Christopherson, & M. A. Bonjean (Eds.), *Aging and family therapy: Practitioner perspectives on Golden Pond* (pp. 47-55). New York: Haworth.

Hughston, D. S., & Hughston, G. A. (1989). Legal ramifications of elderly cohabitation: Necessity for recognition of its implications by family therapists. In G. A. Hughston, V. A. Christopherson, & M. J. Bonjean (Eds.), *Aging and family therapy: Practitioner perspectives on Golden Pond* (pp. 163-172). New York: Haworth.

Imber-Black, I. (1986). Toward a resource model in systemic family therapy. In M. Karpel (Ed.), *Family resources: The hidden partner in family therapy* (pp. 148-174). New York: Guilford.

Jennings, J. (1987). Elderly parents as caregivers for their adult dependent children. *Social Work, 32*, 430-433.

Johnson, V. (1986). *Intervention: How to help someone who doesn't want help.* Minneapolis, MN: Johnson Institute.

Karpel, M. (1986). Testing, promoting, and preserving family resources: Beyond pathology and power. In M. Karpel (Ed.), *Family resources: The hidden partner in family therapy* (pp. 175-234). New York: Guilford.

Keeney, B. (1979). Ecosystemic epistemology: An alternative paradigm for diagnosis. *Family Process, 18*, 117-129.

Keller, J. F., & Bromley, M. C. (1989). Psychotherapy with the elderly: A systemic model. In G. A. Hughston, V. A. Christopherson, & M. A. Bonjean (Eds.), *Aging and family therapy: Practitioner perspectives on Golden Pond* (pp. 29-45). New York: Haworth.

Kramer, J. (1985). *Family interfaces: Transgenerational patterns.* New York: Brunner/Mazel.

Kubler-Ross, E. (1969). *On death and dying.* New York: Macmillan.

Kubler-Ross, E. (1975). *Death: The final stage of growth.* Englewood Cliffs, NJ: Prentice Hall.

Kutner, L. M. (1990, April 1). If parents have problems, should you intervene? *Ann Arbor (Michigan) News*, p. F5.

Lebowitz, B. D. (1985). Family caregiving in old age. *Hospital and Community Psychiatry, 36*, 457-458.

Lewis, C. S. (1961). *A grief observed.* New York: Seabury.

McGoldrick, M. (1982). Normal families: An ethnic perspective. In F. Walsh (Ed.), *Normal family processes* (pp. 399-424). New York: Guilford.

McGoldrick, M., & Gerson, R. (1985). *Genograms in family therapy.* New York: Norton.

McGoldrick, M., Hines, P., Lee, E., & Preto, N. G. (1986, November-December). Mourning rituals. *The Family Therapy Networker, 10*(6), 28-36.

McGoldrick, M., Pearce, J., & Giordano, J. (Eds.). (1982). *Ethnicity and family therapy.* New York: Guilford.

McQuellon, R. P., & Reifler, B. V. (1989). Caring for the depressed elderly and their families. In G. A. Hughston, V. A. Christopherson, & M. J. Bonjean (Eds.), *Aging and family therapy: Practitioner perspectives on Golden Pond* (pp. 97-116). New York: Haworth.

Meth, R., & Pasick, R. (1990). *Men in therapy: The challenge of change.* New York: Guilford.

Miller, D. (1981). The "sandwich generation": Adult children and aging. *Social Work, 26*, 419-423.

Minuchin, S. (1974). *Families & family therapy.* Cambridge, MA: Harvard University Press.

Minuchin, S. (1991, September-October). The seductions of constructivism. *The Family Therapy Networker, 15*(5), 47-50.

Minuchin, S., & Fishman, H. C. (1981). *Family therapy techniques.* Cambridge, MA: Harvard University Press.

Minuchin, S., Rosman, B. L., & Baker, L. (1978). *Psychosomatic families: Anorexia nervosa in context.* Cambridge, MA: Harvard University Press.

Mohr, R., & Frankfurt, M. (1988, July-August). Second careers. *The Family Therapy Networker, 12*(4), 47-51.

Montalvo, B., & Thompson, R. (1988, July-August). Conflicts in the caregiving family. *The Family Therapy Networker, 12*(4), 30-35.

Montgomery, R. J. V., & Datwyler, M. M. (1990). Women and men in the caregiving role. *Generations, 14*(3), 34-38.

Moroney, R. M. (1980). *Families, social services, and social policy: The issue of shared responsibility*. Washington, DC: U.S. Department of Health and Human Services.

Nelson, G. M. (1982). Support for the aged: Public and private responsibility. *Social Work, 27*, 137-143.

O'Connor, T. (1989, September-October). Therapy for a dying planet. *The Family Therapy Networker, 13*(5), 69-72.

Papp, P. (1983). *The process of change*. New York: Guilford.

Peterson, E., & Nelson, K. (1987). How to meet your clients' spiritual needs. *Journal of Psychosocial Nursing, 25*(5), 34-39.

Peterson, J. A. (1973). Marital and family therapy involving the aged. *The Gerontologist, 13*(1), 27-31.

Pillemer, K. A. (1986). Risk factors in elder abuse: Results from a case-control study. In K. A. Pillemer (Ed.), *Elder abuse: Conflict in the family*. Westport, CT: Greenwood.

Pillemer, K. A., & Finkelhor, D. (1988). The prevalence of elder abuse: A random sample survey. *The Gerontological Society of America, 28*(1), 51-57.

Powell, T. J., & Fellin, P. A. (1987). *Mental health services for older adults in Michigan: Progress, problems, and prospects*. Report to State of Michigan Department of Mental Health. Ann Arbor: University of Michigan School of Socal Work.

Rolland, J. S. (1987). Chronic illness and the life cycle: A conceptual framework. *Family Process, 26*(2), 203-221.

Satir, V. (1967). *Conjoint family therapy*. Palo Alto, CA: Science & Behavior Books.

Schuckit, M. A. (1990). Assessment and treatment strategies with the late life alcoholic. *Journal of Geriatric Psychiatry, 23*(2), 83-89.

Selvini Palazzoli, M., Boscolo, L., Cecchin, G. O., & Prata, G. (1980). Hypothesizing — circularity — neutrality: Three guidelines for the conductor of the session. *Family Process, 19*(1), 3-12.

Selvini Palazzoli, M., Cecchin, G., Prata, G., & Boscolo, L. (1978). *Paradox and counterparadox*. New York: Jason Aronson.

Silverman, A. G., Brahce, C. I., & Zielinski, C. (1981). *As parents grow older: A manual for program replication*. Ann Arbor: Institute of Gerontology, University of Michigan.

Soldo, B., & Myllyluoma, J. (1983). Caregivers who live with dependent elderly. *The Gerontologist, 23*, 605-611.

Sprung, G. M. (1989, December). Transferential issues in working with older adults. *Social Casework: The Journal of Contemporary Social Work, 70*(10), 597-602.

Survey shows elderly home care most often provided by spouses. (1985, October). *AARP News Bulletin*, p. 3.

Tilley, K. (1990, January/February). Important to know behaviors of elderly. *Family Therapy News*, p. 8.

Toseland, R. W., Rossiter, C. M., Peak, T., & Smith, G. C. (1990). Comparative effectiveness of individual and group interventions to support family caregivers. *Social Work, 35*(3), 209-217.

U.S. Bureau of the Census. (1989). *Household and family characteristics: March 1988.* (Current Population Reports, Series P-20. No. 437). Washington, DC: Government Printing Office.

Walsh, F. (1980). The family in later life. In E. Carter & M. McGoldrick (Eds.), *The family life cycle: A framework for family therapy* (pp. 197-220). New York: Gardner.

Walsh, F. (Ed.). (1982). *Normal family processes.* New York: Guilford.

Watzlawick, P., Beavin, J., & Jackson, D. (1967). *Pragmatics of human communication.* New York: Norton.

Watzlawick, P., Weakland, J., & Fisch, R. (1974). Change: Principles of problem formation and problem resolution. New York: Norton.

Webster's new collegiate dictionary. (1977). Springfield, MA: G. & C. Merriam.

Whitbourne, S. D. (1990). Sexuality in the aging male. *Generations, 14*(3), 28-30.

White, M., & Epston, D. (1990). *Narrative means to therapeutic ends.* New York: Norton.

Williams, F. R. (1989). Bereavement and the elderly: The role of the psychotherapist. In G. A. Hughston, V. A. Christopherson, & M. J. Bonjean (Eds.), *Aging and family therapy: Practitioner perspectives on Golden Pond* (pp. 225-241). New York: Haworth.

Williamson, D. (1982). Person authority via termination of the intergenerational hierarchical boundary. *Journal of Marital and Family Therapy, 8,* 23-37.

Wilson, V. (1990). The consequences of elderly wives caring for disabled husbands. *Social Work, 35*(5), 417-421.

Yee, B. W. K. (1990). Gender & family issues in minority groups. *Generations, 14*(3), 39-42.

INDEX

ABOUT THE AUTHORS

JO ANN ALLEN is Professor Emeritus of the University of Michigan School of Social Work. She maintains an active practice with individuals, couples, and families as an affiliate of the Ann Arbor Center for the Family and offers continuing education for family therapists through the Ann Arbor Center for Research and Training. In addition to an interest in practice with older adults and their families, her current efforts center on issues of gender. Most recently, she is a contributing author to *Men in Therapy*, edited by Richard Meth and Robert Pasick, and she is coauthor with Kris Kissman of *Single Parent Families*, in press.

PAUL ESTENSON is a clinical psychologist trained at the University of Michigan. He maintains a private practice in affiliation with the Ann Arbor Center for the Family. His interests in substance abuse and the elderly are long-standing. He was the founding director of the Older Adult Chemical Dependency Program at Chelsea (Michigan) Community Hospital, one of the few inpatient programs in the country specializing in the treatment of older substance abusers. He has served as consulting and supervising psychologist to the Older Adult Recovery Center in Ann Arbor, a program offering treatment to substance abusers and family members, and has consulted extensively regarding issues related to handicapped children and their families.

MARILYN L. FLYNN is Director of the School of Social Work at Michigan State University. She received her Ph.D. from the University of Illinois at Urbana, with specializations in social policy and economics. Since 1978 she has consulted to more than 80 for-profit, public, and not-for-profit groups on issues of strategic planning, program evaluation, information systems, and organization design. She is the author of more than 50 book chapters, journal articles, and technical reports. Her current research interest is the design and evaluation of multidisciplinary collaborations serving high need populations in health and human services. She has been working on policy analysis and program implementation for older persons since 1968 and is presently completing a multigenerational study of services in Flint and Genesee County, Michigan.

ELIZABETH R. NEIDHARDT is Clinical Services Supervisor at Hegira Programs, Inc., in Wayne, Michigan, where she directs the outpatient mental health and substance abuse programs. She graduated from Smith College and received her M.S.W. and Certificate in Management/Administration from the University of Michigan School of Social Work. She has held clinical supervisory positions at family service agencies and community mental health centers where she focused on family therapy and the needs of the elderly. She has presented papers and workshops nationally on the subject of family therapy as it applies to work with the elderly. Ms. Neidhardt maintains an active private practice in family, marital, and individual therapy.

Family Therapy
With the
Elderly

SAGE SOURCEBOOKS FOR THE HUMAN SERVICES SERIES

Series Editors: ARMAND LAUFFER and CHARLES GARVIN

Recent Volumes in this Series